We Believe For Kids!

Quarter 1

Who is God?

Teacher's Guide

We Believe For Kids!
Teacher's Guide

Rev. Randall A. Bach, General Editor
Dr. David L. Cole, Theological Editor
Rev. Andrea P. Johnson, Copy Editor

Copyright © 2021 by OBC Publishing
Published in Des Moines, Iowa, by OBC Publishing

Color version ISBN: 978-1-7373442-0-9

Printed in the United States of America.

Contents

Acknowledgments

Teachers, we appreciate you! You understand the importance of investing your time into our children, giving them a sound spiritual basis by which they can develop an informed, faith-filled worldview. Your dedication will help steer the course of their lives.

We are indebted to a team of knowledgeable, dedicated children's workers, youth workers, and other leaders with a wealth of experience in teaching and leading student ministries who voluntarily worked diligently to help envision, craft, and write the curriculum for *We Believe For Kids*. They are:

Rev. Randall A. Bach   **Kelly Loftis**
Rev. Hannah J. Bemis   **Claudine Morgan-Lewis**
Rev. Chris Cavan   **Rev. Kevin Starkey**
Rev. Candi Hagan   **Taylor Van Sickle**
Rev. Andrea Johnson

We also appreciate the many people who have made this book a reality. We offer a huge "thank you" to **Nicole Kerr**, our creative assistant, for her immense contributions, including creating the *Student's Journal* and for contributing to the graphic design and layout. Her imaginative and administrative skills have driven and shaped this entire process from its inception to its completion. We also want to call out **Hannah Bemis**, for the hours she spent proofreading in addition to hours of writing. We are also grateful to **Greg Roberts**, Open Bible's print media manager, for graphic design, layout, and publishing research.

We want to credit **Lucas Hansen** for the cover and book design concept and **Paula Hernández**, a freelance illustrator and concept artist with Boomi Art, for creating our superhero mascots, Centro and Nora.

Finally, we thank churches like yours that recognize the fact that we have a huge opportunity and responsibility to communicate to our young people the importance of living out their faith in Christ and to give them tools to do so. May God continue the work He has called you to do.

Randall A. Bach, David L. Cole, and Andrea P. Johnson

Introduction

Have you thought about why you do some of the things you do, why you make some of the choices you make, or support some of the causes you support?

Social media, your teachers, your parents, and others are all trying to tell you what to do; they even try to tell you how to think! Some of those voices are pretty loud, and they don't always agree. How do you know which of these voices to listen to? Are you one that follows the crowd, or do you like to think things through on your own?

You may have heard of **The Emperor's New Clothes**, a folktale written by Hans Christian Andersen. In the story a couple of swindlers manage to talk a vain emperor into buying expensive clothing from them that is supposedly invisible to those who are "stupid" or "incompetent." The emperor loves the idea, and the fraudsters proceed to display what they describe as exquisite bolts of cloth with which they pretend to create elaborate clothing.

Of course the whole thing is a hoax, but the emperor does not let on that he cannot see the clothing because he doesn't want people to think he is incompetent. All the townspeople as well ooh and aah over the clothing because they too fear being thought of as inept. In the end, the emperor is left parading before the whole village in nothing but his underclothes!

Sadly, this scenario has played out in much of our society today. Many people try to get us to go along with the crowd and to follow the latest trends even though those trends may be wrong. The emperor may have believed he was wearing fine clothing, but in reality, he was nearly naked. We too may want to believe certain things are true but that does not make them true, even if everyone else thinks they are.

That's why it is important that you know what truth is. Real truth does not change. Real truth helps us make right decisions. More important, real truth leads us to God.

We want to help you discover truth. That's why we are so excited to share with you *We Believe For Kids!* This course will help you answer questions such as "Who is God?" "Who Am I?" and "Why Am I Here?" This course is designed to present you with information that will help you make your own decisions about what you believe, and to make those decisions based on truth. This journal will help you remember the information you are taught and also provide a place to record your own thoughts and opinions. We encourage you to keep it even after you have completed the course as a way to look back and remember your thought processes at this time.

More than anything, we trust that you will use this class time to deepen your relationship with God. He really wants to spend time with you!

Randall A. Bach, David L. Cole, and Andrea P. Johnson

We Believe For Kids!

Teacher's Guide

Lesson 1
"The Bible"

Lesson 1

Doctrinal Statement:

We believe the Bible is God's Word; it is truth. It serves as a trustworthy guide to our everyday lives.

Big Question:

Why should I believe the Bible?

Lesson Aim:

To lay a foundation of understanding that the Bible is true and can be relied on.

Key Verse:

"All Scripture is inspired by God and is useful to teach us what is true and to make us realize what is wrong in our lives. It corrects us when we are wrong and teaches us to do what is right" (2 Timothy 3:16).

Materials:

A physical Bible for each student
Student's journals

The Bible

Setup:

Make sure every student has a physical copy of a Bible. Choose two students to act out the script printed in their workbooks.

Warming Up: [5 minutes]

Welcome students. Pray together as you begin class. Ask that God would lead the discussion times, and that He would put a love in your hearts for His Word and for truth.

Lesson 1

Questions: [5 minutes]

Ask the students:

What are your favorite movies?

How many of them are based on books?

Are any of your favorites based on true stories?

What makes movies and books that are based on true stories so powerful?

Skit: [5 minutes]

Full script in the back of teachers guide (page 170) and student workbook (page 134).

Important facts:

Diary of a Wimpy Kid - sold over 200 million copies
Narnia - sold over 100 million copies
Lord of the Rings - sold over 150 million copies
Harry Potter - sold over 500 million copies
The Holy Bible - sold over 5 billion copies
*(every year 100 million are sold or given away,
translated into more languages than any other book)*

Going Deeper: [15 minutes]

Let's take a look at our doctrinal statement.

"Doctrine" simply means something we believe that is based on what the Bible says.

Each of our lessons will have a statement like this.

Today's statement says, **"We believe the Bible is God's Word; it is truth. It serves as a trustworthy guide to our everyday lives."**

Do you believe this is true? Do you think everything in the Bible is true? Why or why not? *Discuss for a while.*

We saw in the skit that the Bible has been the most popular book for many, many years. It's even more popular than some of the most popular fiction or fantasy books for kids today.

Why do you think that is?
Let the kids discuss for a bit.

Even though fiction books (books that are not true) are entertaining, and can captivate our attention for a short time, there's something special about a book that is 100 percent true. Just like we talked about in the beginning of class,

Lesson 1

some of the most powerful movies are based on true stories. We can look at true stories for examples of how problems have been solved by other, real people. We can learn from others' mistakes. We can be inspired by incredible stories that have actually happened. This is true about any true story.

But what makes the Bible even more special?

Let's actually turn to the Bible to answer this question about the Bible!

Ask if there is a volunteer who feels comfortable looking up 2 Timothy 3:16.

2 Timothy 3:16:
All Scripture is inspired by God and is useful to teach us what is true and to make us realize what is wrong in our lives. It corrects us when we are wrong and teaches us to do what is right.

We can see in this Scripture why the Bible is so important and all the ways we can use it. No wonder it's so popular.

But you also see in this Scripture why we can count on it being true. It's actually inspired by God. In other words, He wrote it!

8

The Bible

Christians believe the Bible is 100 percent the creation of human authors but also 100 percent inspired by God. How is that possible?

Refer to the picture of the Eiffel Tower in student book:

Who's heard of the Eiffel Tower? It's a landmark in Paris, France, built in the late 1880s. It's huge — 1,063 feet tall (the size of an 81-story building).

Can you guess how many pieces of steel were needed to build this? (18,038).

Maurice Koechlin was the lead designer. He created over 5,000 drawings to help the construction workers know what to do. He didn't fabricate or install any of the 18,038 parts, but no one would deny that he was the inspiration behind it all.

Without him it couldn't have been done; it would never have been created.

Similarly, the Bible was written by many different writers but there was one designer, one inspiration behind it all: God himself.

Hold up a Bible.

God himself breathed this Truth into existence. He planted the words in the minds of many writers, helping them create this book that is capable of guiding us when we are lost, revealing God's love for us and transforming our lives.

Lots of people have written good, even inspirational works that did not make it into the Bibles we now hold in our hands.

The material that we find in our Bibles underwent intense scrutiny over time by recognized, biblical scholars and church leaders who made sure that the material that would be included in the Bible you now have in front of you was inspired by the Holy Spirit.

To be included among the books in the New Testament, the book's author must have been an apostle or have a close connection with an apostle. If a person was one of Jesus' twelve disciples or an important Christian teaching, like Paul, who encountered Jesus on the road to Damascus (Acts 9), that person was considered an apostle. Second, the book must have been accepted by the body of Christ at large. Third, the book had to contain consistency of doctrine and orthodox teaching. Orthodox teaching is teaching that conforms to what is generally or traditionally accepted as right or true. Finally, the book had to bear evidence of high moral and spiritual values that would reflect a work of the Holy Spirit as the divine Author.

The books in the Old Testament were written by authors who were led by the Holy Spirit, were collected, and had been a part of the worship lives of Jewish believers for centuries, up until the era of Jesus and His apostles. Those 39 books, along with our 27 New Testament books, were received as Holy Scriptures, as the inspired and authoritative Word of God for believers in the early church.

God, in His sovereignty, brought the early church leaders to the recognition of the books He had inspired, and those books are in the Bible you now hold. But don't just take their word for it.

Ask another student to look up John 14:6.

John 14:6:
Jesus told him, I am the way, the truth and the life. No one can come to the Father except through me.

Jesus says right here that He is the truth. We're going to learn more about Jesus in later lessons, but as you might already know, we believe Jesus is God in human form. So if Jesus and God are truth, then it makes sense that anything they create must be true.

The Bible doesn't just contain some things that are true; **it IS truth!** You can count on Jesus and on His Word. The more you read it, the more you will recognize its truth and experience its power in your lives.

Lesson 1

Activation: [15 minutes]

Distribute a Bible to each student.

The Bible is a collection of books printed together.

The term "Bible" is from the Latin word "biblia," which means a library or collection of books. Look at the index of the names of all the books.

There are two main sections: the Old Testament and the New Testament.

Have them turn the pages. Help them find the Old and New Testaments. Tell them to feel the difference in size between the two.

The Bible

Important fact:

The Old Testament is the larger of the two testaments and includes everything from the creation of the world until just a few hundred years before Jesus.

Important fact:

The first four books of the New Testament are called the gospels. They are firsthand accounts of the life of Jesus. The rest of the New Testament recounts how the early followers of Jesus were instructed to live and follow Jesus' teachings.

Important fact:

The Bible was written over a time span of 1,600 years by at least 40 authors, which included kings, scholars, tax collectors, philosophers, fishermen, statesmen, poets, historians, teachers, prophets, and doctors.

Lesson 1

Important fact:

The Bible contains different types of literature: history, poetry, prophecy, and even letters. More than 300 prophetic details (details mentioned before they actually happened) about Jesus' life found in the Old Testament came true, such as the fact that He would be born of a virgin, His birthplace would be Bethlehem, and that He would be crucified between two thieves.

There are places in the world where it is illegal to do exactly what you are doing, holding a Bible. There are real people, missionaries in Open Bible, who risk their lives to get Bibles into the hands of people who aren't allowed to read it. There are people who are killed for simply having a Bible in their possession.

Why do you think these people risk their lives to read it?

Why do you think it is so precious to them?

Pause to let students answer.

It is precious to them because it is truth. The Bible is the answer. It's life to them. Just like Jesus, this book you hold in your hands is the way, the truth, and the life. There is nothing more precious.

Closing: [15 minutes]

Final Journal Activity:

What did you learn or discover about the Bible today?

What is your most precious possession? Draw a picture or write about it.

What is one small goal you can set to make the Bible a bigger part of your life?

Discuss their responses if time.

Close in prayer.

Extra game idea: Have students play Pictionary to illustrate their precious possessions. This game could take place earlier in the lesson or at the end.

We Believe For Kids!

Teacher's Guide

Lesson 2
"The Bible"

Lesson 2

Doctrinal Statement:

We believe the Bible is God's Word; it is truth. It serves as a trustworthy guide to our everyday lives.

Big Question:

Why should the Bible matter to me?

Lesson Aim:

To show students that the Bible is alive and written for us; it has the power to transform our lives.

Key Verse:

"For the word of God is alive and powerful. It is sharper than the sharpest two-edged sword, cutting between soul and spirit, between joint and marrow. It exposes our innermost thoughts and desires" (Hebrews 4:12).

Materials:

A physical Bible for each student
Student's journals

Materials: (cont.)

White board or butcher paper
Balloons
Darts or pins
Slips of paper printed with encouraging Scriptures. Samples:

Isaiah 12:2	Isaiah 43:1-2	Isaiah 58:11
Jeremiah 29:11	Jeremiah 33:3	Psalm 139:1-3
Romans 12:21	Philippians 1:9	Philippians 4:6-7
Ephesians 1:17-19	Ephesians 3:16-19	1 Timothy 4:12
2 Timothy 1:7		

Setup:

Divide a white board or butcher paper into two columns with the following headings: "Powerful" and "Personal."

Write encouraging verses on slips of paper (see list above) and insert them into the balloons. (Pray that God will divinely match each student with the perfect verse.) Then blow up the balloons.

Lesson 2

Warming Up: [5 minutes]

Welcome students. Open with prayer, asking that God would speak personally to each student today.

Ask for volunteers to find and be ready to read our key Scriptures. (Alternatively, print verses out ahead of time and ask students to read them at designated times.)

Review the doctrinal statement together. Remind students of last week's lesson, how we established that the Bible is true and reliable. Explain that this week we're going to learn about two other qualities of the Bible: it is powerful and personal.

Display the white board or butcher paper divided into two columns: Powerful and Personal. Ask students to share or come forward and write in each column what the heading makes them think of.

For example: "Powerful" = superheroes, muscles, strong; Personal = mine, just for me, about a person.

Going Deeper: [20 minutes]

One of the things we might think of when we hear the word "powerful" is a powerful weapon. A lot of powerful figures have weapons, right? Superheroes, policemen, or soldiers…
Take other examples from students.

Did you guys know that we've been given a weapon by God?
Give students a chance to answer.
Yep, we've been given a sword!

Have the first student read aloud

Hebrews 4:12:
For the word of God is alive and powerful. It is sharper than the sharpest two-edged sword, cutting between soul and spirit, between joint and marrow. It exposes our innermost thoughts and desires.

Lesson 2

Have the second student read aloud

Ephesians 6:17:
Put on salvation as your helmet, and take the sword of the Spirit, which is the word of God.

So, what is our sword? **The Word of God.** And what is the Word of God? **The Bible.** Do you guys believe that the Bible is actually as powerful as the sharpest sword imaginable?

Let's dig deeper in Hebrews 4:12. What might it mean to cut between soul and spirit or between joint and marrow?

How hard is it to cut these things apart?

What kinds of special tools do surgeons or doctors use?

In Ephesians 6:17 we find out that God's Word is our main weapon for battle. It's part of the armor of God, but you know what's interesting? It's the only offensive weapon listed. Everything else (helmet, shield, etc.) serves to protect us, but the Word of God is how we attack our enemy. Who are we attacking or fighting? ***Have students look further into Ephesians 6 to find the answer.*** How can we use God's Word to attack the enemy and fight battles in our lives?

The Bible

Ask a third student to read aloud

2 Timothy 3:16:
All Scripture is inspired by God and is useful to teach us what is true and to make us realize what is wrong in our lives. It corrects us when we are wrong and teaches us to do what is right.

You may even want to establish that Scripture = the Bible.

Let's talk about the idea of Scripture being inspired. Some versions use the term "God-breathed."

How powerful must God's breath be?

What kinds of things happen when God breathes on something?

Let students lead the discussion, but eventually reveal the truth that when God breathes, things come to life!

You can refer to the following verses:

Genesis 2:7:
Then the LORD God formed the man from the dust of the ground. He breathed the breath of life into the man's nostrils, and the man became a living person.

Lesson 2

Ezekiel 37:5:
This is what the Sovereign Lord says: Look! I am going to put breath into you and make you live again!

Job 33:4:
For the Spirit of God has made me, and the breath of the Almighty gives me life.

When something is God-breathed, it is alive! God's breath is so powerful that it brings dead things back to life and turns dirt into a masterpiece. That means the words in this book aren't just words. **Hold up Bible.** They have the power to bring you to life and help turn you into the masterpiece God made you to be.

What else, or actually Who else do we know that could bring dead things back to life using only His words? **Jesus!**.

Some examples are Tabitha **(Acts 9:36-41)** and Lazarus **(John 11:1-44).**

The Bible

Have a student read aloud

John 1:1-4:
In the beginning the Word already existed. The Word was with God, and the Word was God. He existed in the beginning with God. God created everything through him, and nothing was created except through him. The Word gave life to everything that was created, and his life brought light to everyone.

So these verses are describing the term the "Word" again, but it doesn't seem like we're talking about a book. The verses describe the Word like it's a person.

Who could this verse be describing?

Read

John 1:14:
So the Word became human and made his home among us.

We know that the Bible is made of God's breath and that it can bring people to life. We know that Jesus can bring people to life. Now we see that Jesus and the Bible have a name in common: the Word.

Lesson 2

When God sent Jesus to us, it was another way for Him to send His very words to us, everything He wanted to tell us and share with us. When Jesus spoke, He spoke God's words. When we read the Bible, we read God's words.

We talked about how the Bible is personal, and here is why: the Bible, just like Jesus, was sent to you from God.

The Bible is full of messages from God to you.

This book, breathed into existence by God, is also the essence of Jesus. If you want to get to know Jesus better, look right here.

If you want to know who God made you to be or what He thinks of you, this is the only book you need. *This book tells you who you really are; then it gives you the power to become that person.*

Have a student read aloud

Psalm 119:105:
Your Word is a lamp to guide my feet and a light for my path.

Do you notice the word "my" in the verse? The Bible was written to help guide you. It's personal. It's yours.

Activation: [20 minutes]

In the following activity, students use darts or pins to pop balloons. Alternatively, students can randomly select a balloon from a big bag and pop it, or the teacher can hide the balloons in an area and the first one a student finds is theirs to pop, etc. There are many ways to adapt this activity!

We're going to do an activity to demonstrate how personal God's Word is. Inside each of these balloons is a verse that I believe is a personal message from God just for you. I have prayed that God will use His power to direct each of you to the balloon with the verse that was meant for you today. You are going to be given a dart (or pin) and one at a time, you will throw your dart at the balloon board *(change directions based on how you decide to proceed with the activity)*.

Whichever balloon your dart pops is going to be your word from God today. Here's the catch: Inside your balloon you will only find the Scripture reference (for example, John 3:16). You will get to practice becoming familiar with the Bible as you look up and find your verse. Once you find it, I want you to do two things. First, I want you to pray that God will speak to you and show you what He is saying to you through the verse. He will speak! Then, I want you to write down both the verse and everything you hear Him saying to you. There is space on your student page to respond in this way today.

Lesson 2

Be ready to facilitate the activity and be flexible. The main goal is that all students end up with a balloon that they can pop; how you get to that point isn't so important. Also be prepared to help students look up their Scriptures, and to encourage students who might feel intimidated or frustrated if they don't hear from God right away.

Remind them that God has promised to give His Spirit to guide us as we read, and that He has promised that we can hear His voice (John 10:27).

Sometimes it just takes practice; it's okay if they don't hear anything this time. After all students have popped their balloons, it might be helpful to play some quiet worship music to transition into the reflecting and writing time.

Teachers are encouraged to spend some time in prayer the week before this lesson is taught, asking God which Scriptures to place inside the balloons. Pray that God will divinely match each student with the perfect verse, and that each student will hear His voice and encounter His love for them.

When the activity is finished, see if any students feel comfortable sharing what God spoke to them. If not, that's okay. Don't pressure students to share.

Closing: [15 minutes]

So, what did we learn about God's Word today? *Allow students to answer.*

God's Word is personal and powerful. The Bible was written from God to each of us, and it has the power to individually guide us and transform our lives. Why wouldn't we want to read such an incredible book?

I have two challenges for you this week. You can pick one or do both.

Challenge 1: Read your Bible, at least one verse, every day this week. Then, write down what you hear God saying to you through that verse. I'd love to hear what God's been speaking to you when I see you next week!

If you have time, let students practice this, using one of the verses from this lesson.

Challenge 2: Memorize the verse that was in your balloon today. Share it with me next week! *You can use this time to play one of the memory verse games listed in the front of the book.*

Close in prayer. Pray that God will bless the students to hear from God as they read their Bibles this week. Also pray over any personal requests they have.

We Believe For Kids!

Teacher's Guide

Lesson 3
"The Bible"

Lesson 3

Doctrinal Statement:

We believe the Bible is God's Word; it is truth. It serves as a trustworthy guide to our everyday lives.

Big Question:

How is the Bible useful for me today?

Lesson Aim:

To let students know that the Bible guides us in our everyday lives.

Key Verse:

"Your word is a lamp to guide my feet and a light for my path" (Psalm 119:105).

Materials:

A physical Bible for each student

Student's journals

Laptop or other screen queued up to the link in Setup section.

Materials: (cont.)

Examples of student Bible-reading plans and daily devotional books such as
- *Unseen: The Prince Warriors 365 Devotionals,* by Priscilla Shirer
- *Jesus Calling: 365 Devotions for Kids,* by Sarah Young.
(Bible plans are available at The Bible App: YouVersion).

Setup:

Locate the video "How to Read the Bible" preferably to be projected to a screen for all students to watch easily.

Watch Youtube video, *"How do I read the Bible?"*
at https://youtu.be/-ADbU6fMG6A

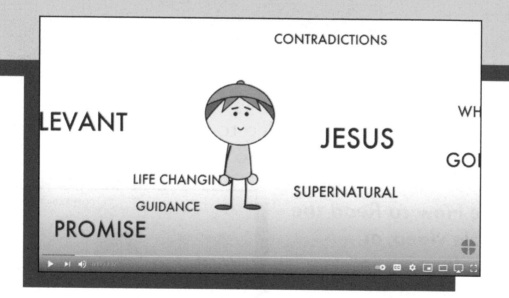

Lesson 3

Warming Up: [20 minutes]

Open with prayer or ask if a student would be comfortable opening in prayer.

Remind students about last week's teaching. Review how the Bible is alive and how it has the power to transform our lives. Give students a chance to share the verse that they were challenged to memorize. Ask if anyone would like to share something God spoke to them through that verse.

So we know the Bible can transform our lives, but it's hard for it to transform our lives if we never read it, right? But how do we start reading it? Diving into such a huge book can be overwhelming, especially if we feel like we don't understand it.

Has anyone ever felt like the Bible is too big or too hard or too boring to read?

You're not alone. I have a short video to show you guys about someone else who found it difficult to read the Bible.

Watch the How to Read the Bible video, at https://youtu.be/-ADbU6fMG6A.

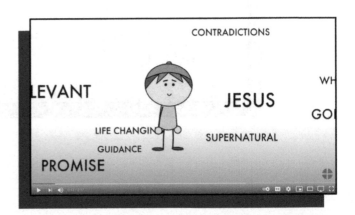

The Bible

Follow up with some discussion.

Just like Bob in the video, there are a lot of great strategies for reading the Bible. We're going to talk about a few of them today. But I'll tell you a secret about understanding the Bible: It's less about how you read it and more about Who you read it with.

The most powerful thing you can do to help yourself understand God's Word is to invite the Holy Spirit to read it with you.

Ask for volunteers to find and be ready to share the key verses for today's lesson:

Psalm 119:18, Jeremiah 33:3, John 14:26, 1 John 2:27.

Alternatively, print out key verses and ask students to read them at the designated times throughout the lesson.

Lesson 3

Going Deeper: [15 minutes]

Let's read our first verse together,

Psalm 119:18:
Open my eyes to see the wonderful truths in your instructions.

What are the "instructions" the writer of the Psalm is talking about?

Discuss until students identify that the "instructions" are the Bible.

The writer of this Psalm knew what we know today: The Bible is too hard to understand alone. We need God to open our eyes to understand what we read. If we ask God to do this, He promises that He will help.

Let's read Jeremiah 33:3.

Jeremiah 33:3:
Ask me and I will tell you remarkable secrets you do not know. . . .

The Bible

God tells us right here, just ask! He's excited to share his secrets with us. He wants to speak to us and help us understand what He is saying.

The Bible isn't something our brain can understand all by itself. It was written not just for our brains, but also for our spirit.

Important fact:

Our spirit is the nonphysical part of our being.
It's the part of us that holds our emotions and character.
It's the part that will remain alive after our body dies,
the part that connects to God.

Let's try something. I'm going to read a passage of Scripture out loud to you, and I want you to close your eyes, listen, and just see how you feel as I read it to you.

Read the 23rd Psalm to the students.

If you have a particularly active group and you know this exercise will not work for them, you can skip it. But try to challenge students to take this seriously and quiet themselves to listen.

Lesson 3

Psalm 23:
The Lord is my shepherd; I have all that I need.

He lets me rest in green meadows; he leads me beside peaceful streams.

He renews my strength. He guides me along right paths, bringing honor to his name.

Even when I walk through the darkest valley, I will not be afraid, for you are close beside me. Your rod and your staff protect and comfort me.

You prepare a feast for me in the presence of my enemies. You honor me by anointing my head with oil. My cup overflows with blessings.

Surely your goodness and unfailing love will pursue me all the days of my life, and I will live in the house of the Lord forever.

The Bible

How did you feel as you listened to this passage?

Allow students to answer.

Often, even when we don't fully understand what the Bible's words mean, we can still feel calm and peaceful as we read or listen to it.

That's because your spirit understands God's Word on a level that your brain doesn't. The Holy Spirit can speak to your spirit and allow your emotions and thoughts to be blessed by God's Word.

Let's read a couple more Scriptures that promise we will have help when we read the Bible.

Call on pre-arranged students to read each of the following Scriptures

John 14:26:
But when the Father sends the Advocate as my representative – that is, the Holy Spirit – he will teach you everything and will remind you of everything I have told you.

1 John 2:27:
But you have received the Holy Spirit, and he lives within you, so you don't need anyone to teach you what is true. For the Spirit teaches you everything you need to know....

Lesson 3

What do you hear these verses saying?

Who is our helper when it comes to understanding the Bible?

Activation: [20 minutes]

Okay, so now that we know "Who," let's talk about "How."

How can we use the Bible today? What are some strategies to help us start reading this big book so it can transform us?

We saw a few ideas in the beginning video, such as listening to the Bible on an app or recording or reading the Bible with others.

But I'd love to hear from you! Maybe you've already found some strategies that work for you when you read your Bible.

Does anyone want to share some ways you read your Bible?

Give students a chance to respond.

The Bible

There are so many great ways to read the Bible. I'm going to give you three ideas, and then we're going to practice one of them together.

1. Use a reading plan or a devotional.

These are nice because they give you the exact amount you need to read each day. Sometimes it's hard to know where to start or how much to read, but books or plans like this can guide you.

Pass around examples of daily devotional books so students can get their hands on them and look through them to see what they are like.

The problem with reading plans is that sometimes they feel like too much. You never need to feel guilty if you get behind in your reading. You can always start where you left off. But if your reading plan feels like too much reading for one day, let's talk about another option.

2. Read through one book at a time, as slowly as you need to.

Sometimes it's great to read just one or two verses a day and think about them all day long. This way of reading gives you the flexibility to read at your own pace, but still gives you structure as you read through one book at a time (for example, the book of Mark like in our video).

Lesson 3

3. Ask the Holy Spirit to guide you and choose a verse or a passage at random.

This can be a fun way to shake things up if reading has felt a little boring. It's also a great way to practice hearing God's voice.

Simply pray and ask the Holy Spirit to guide your hands and your eyes, open your Bible, point to a verse, and read! Sometimes it will seem like the verse means nothing, but I challenge you to write it down and pray about it anyway. God can speak to us through even the craziest of verses!

Regardless of what method you choose, there is one thing that is so important: Journal what you read and what God speaks to you through your reading.

Writing things down may feel like schoolwork, but I promise you that when you look back on your journaling, you will be amazed at how much and how often you hear God's voice.

There are so many fun ways to journal! You can draw what you read, you can write a verse in fancy or artistic letters, or you can paint.

There's one very popular way to journal that I want to cover today.

Has anyone ever heard of the SOAP method of Bible journaling?

Allow students to answer, then discuss the following:

S: Scripture - Write down the Scripture passage you read for the day.

O: Observation - What do you notice about the verse? Do you have questions?

A: Application - How might this verse or story apply to your life or what you're going through today?

P: Pray - This is the fun part. Ask God if there's anything else He wants you to know and write down anything you hear Him saying. Thank Him for what He has spoken to you. Ask Him for help or tell Him you're sorry for ways you may have fallen short that came to your mind as you read.

Lesson 3

OK, I promised we would practice and that's what we're going to do now. I want you to get with a partner.

Teacher, feel free to assign partners if this works better for your group.

With your partner, practice the third method we talked about today.

Together, you will pray that the Holy Spirit will guide your hands and eyes to a verse that will speak to you.

One at a time, close your eyes and point to a verse.

Write that verse down in your journal.

Once each of you have done this and written down your own verse, quietly spend some time journaling about that verse using the "SOAP" method.

44

Closing: [5 minutes]

What did you hear from God through His Word today?

Is anyone brave enough to share your verse and what you felt like God spoke to you through it?

Did anyone get anything that just didn't make sense at all?

Discuss how this is okay.

God's Word will not always make sense; it takes practice to learn to understand and hear His voice. Even the most intelligent biblical scholars still don't understand everything.

What are some of your main take-aways today? What did you learn?

Lesson 3

What is your favorite way to read the Bible that we talked about today?

Which one would you be most likely to try?

Discuss.

Even if you just read one verse a day, staying in communication with God by reading his Word and praying is the best way to grow closer to Him and help your spirit get stronger and more powerful.

With God's Word you can fight against any attack Satan or the world throws at you.

Why wouldn't we want to use this weapon?

Close in prayer.

Ask that God would awaken a passion in the students' hearts for the Word of God.

Ask that He would open their eyes and their spirits to understand what He speaks to them through the Bible.

Thank Him for his faithfulness and his great plans for each one of these students.

We Believe For Kids!

Teacher's Guide

Lesson 4
Review

Lesson 4

Doctrinal Statement:

We believe the Bible is God's Word; it is truth. It serves as a trust-worthy guide to our everyday lives.

Review Big Questions:

Why should I believe the Bible?

Why should the Bible matter to me?

How is the Bible useful for me today?

Lesson Aim:

Review lessons 1, 2, and 3 on the Bible.

Materials:

A physical Bible for each student

Student's journals

Review Lesson 1: The Bible

Doctrinal Statement:

We believe the Bible is God's Word; it is truth. It serves as a trustworthy guide to our everyday lives.

Key Verse:

"All Scripture is inspired by God and is useful to teach us what is true and to make us realize what is wrong in our lives. It corrects us when we are wrong and teaches us to do what is right" (2 Timothy 3:16).

Main Points:

- Even though fiction books (books that are not true) are entertaining, and can captivate our attention for a short time, there's something special about a book that is 100 percent true.

- Christians believe the Bible is 100 percent the creation of human authors but also 100 percent inspired by God.

- God himself breathed this Truth into existence. He planted the words in the minds of many writers, helping them create this book that is capable of guiding us when we are lost, revealing God's love for us and transforming our lives.

- There are two main sections: the Old Testament and the New Testament.

Lesson 4

- The Old Testament is the larger of the two testaments and includes everything from the creation of the world until just a few hundred years before Jesus.

- The first four books of the New Testament are called the gospels. They are firsthand accounts of the life of Jesus. The rest of the New Testament recounts how the early followers of Jesus were instructed to live and follow Jesus' teachings.

- The Bible was written over a time span of 1,600 years by at least 40 authors, which included kings, scholars, tax collectors, philosophers, fishermen, statesmen, poets, historians, teachers, prophets, and doctors.

- The Bible contains different types of literature: history, poetry, prophecy, and even letters. More than 300 prophetic details (details mentioned before they actually happened) about Jesus' life found in the Old Testament came true, such as the fact that He would be born of a virgin, His birthplace would be Bethlehem, and that He would be crucified between two thieves.

Review

Review Lesson 2: The Bible

Doctrinal Statement:

We believe the Bible is God's Word; it is truth. It serves as a trust-worthy guide to our everyday lives.

Key Verse:

"For the word of God is alive and powerful. It is sharper than the sharpest two-edged sword, cutting between soul and spirit, be-tween joint and marrow. It exposes our innermost thoughts and desires" (Hebrews 4:12).

Main Points:

- The Bible is powerful.

- God's Word is our main weapon for battle. It's part of the armor of God (Ephesians 6:17).

- "Scripture" is another word for "Bible."

- Scripture is inspired or "God-breathed."

- God's breath is so powerful that it brings dead things back to life and turns dirt into a masterpiece. That means the words in the Bible aren't just words. They have the power to bring you to life and help turn you into the masterpiece God made you to be.

- When God sent Jesus to us, it was another way for Him to send His very words to us, everything He wanted to tell us and share with us. When Jesus spoke, He spoke God's words. When we read the Bible, we read God's words.

- The Bible is personal. If you want to know who God made you to be or what He thinks of you, this is the only book you need.

Review Lesson 3: The Bible

Doctrinal Statement:

We believe the Bible is God's Word; it is truth. It serves as a trustworthy guide to our everyday lives.

Key Verse:

Psalm 119:105:
Your word is a lamp to guide my feet and a light for my path.

Main Points:

• The most powerful thing you can do to help yourself understand God's Word is to invite the Holy Spirit to read it with you.

• The Bible isn't something our brain can understand all by itself. It was written not just for our brains, but also for our spirit.

• Our spirit is the nonphysical part of our being. It's the part of us that holds our emotions and character. It's the part that will remain alive after our body dies, the part that connects to God.

• There are so many great ways to read the Bible. This lesson gave you three ideas: Reading plans or devotionals, reading through one book at a time, and choosing a random passage to read as th Holy Spirit leads you.

Lesson 4

Reading plan or a devotional -

These are nice because they give you the exact amount you need to read each day.
Sometimes it's hard to know where to start or how much to read, but books or plans like this can guide you.

• Read through one book at a time -

Sometimes it's great to read just one or two verses a day and think about them all day long. This way of reading gives you the flexibility to read at your own pace, but still gives you structure as you read through one book at a time.

• Ask the Holy Spirit to guide you -

Simply pray and ask the Holy Spirit to guide your hands and your eyes, open your Bible, point to a verse, and read! Sometimes it will seem like the verse means nothing, but write it down and pray about it anyway. God can speak to us through even the craziest of verses!

Regardless of what method you choose, there is one thing that is so important: Journal what you read and what God speaks to you through your reading. One popular way to journal is the **SOAP** method.

Scripture - Write down the Scripture passage you read for the day.

Observation - What do you notice about the verse? Do you have questions?

Application - How might this verse or story apply to your life or what you're going through today?

Pray - Ask God if there's anything else He wants you to know and write down anything you hear Him saying. Thank Him for what He has spoken to you.

Review

Review Questions:

These are the answers to the fill in the blank questions in the Student's Journals.

1. **Doctrine** is something we believe that is based on what the Bible says.

1. The Bible is the **best-selling** book of the year, every year!

1. Christians believe that the Bible is 100% the creation of human authors but also 100% **inspired** by God.

1. The Bible is not a random collection of writings, it's God's message of **love** to the world!

1. The Bible is a **collection** of books printed together.

1. "Bible" is from the Latin work "biblia," which means "**library**" or "collection of books".

1. The Bible has two main sections: the **Old Testament**, which is the larger of the two and includes everything from the creation of the world until a few hundred years before Jesus; and the **New Testament**, which includes firsthand accounts of Jesus and how the early followers of Jesus were instructed to live and follow His teachings.

Lesson 4

1. The Bible is a **powerful** weapon that we use to attack our enemy (Satan).

1. The Bible was not just for people thousands of years ago, it is for you, it is **personal**.

1. The first four books of the New Testament are called the **gospels**.

1. Our **spirit** is the nonphysical part of our being that holds our emotions and character. It is the part that connects with God.

1. The **Holy Spirit** is our helper when it comes to understanding the Bible.

1. We talked about different methods for studying the Bible included the SOAP method. SOAP stands for **Scripture**, **Observation**, **Application**, **Prayer**.

1. The doctrinal statement for these last few weeks states that, "We believe the Bible is God's Word; it is **truth**. It serves as a **trustworthy** guide to our everyday lives.

Review

Word Search:

Students will use the answers to the review quetions and find the words in the word search. Answers are below.

Q	L	B	F	S	F	E	V	Z	V	C	S	D	B	B	X	C	E	Q	Y	H	V	U	H	L
Q	L	F	S	G	T	X	P	E	M	O	C	P	S	J	E	I	A	A	L	K	L	U	F	F
H	X	U	C	J	J	V	L	U	R	R	D	U	S	K	H	S	O	L	S	Q	H	B	F	P
N	T	X	I	W	X	N	V	X	F	R	G	Q	R	E	B	F	T	X	R	Z	D	T	P	U
B	R	I	Q	K	F	M	D	I	G	F	M	H	W	G	R	P	S	S	Q	V	A	K	L	L
V	U	T	C	Q	Y	B	G	U	T	B	C	S	Z	T	D	I	N	I	E	G	N	X	Y	C
K	S	F	P	N	Y	E	J	G	O	S	P	E	L	S	F	Z	S	S	T	L	M	P	E	D
S	T	H	G	U	E	X	Q	U	S	P	I	R	I	T	P	R	A	Y	E	R	L	A	J	H
K	W	K	L	I	B	R	A	R	Y	P	V	G	S	H	A	H	U	M	Z	J	B	I	R	H
W	O	C	R	R	P	A	S	J	K	X	Y	E	D	V	H	P	K	S	R	F	I	W	N	W
J	R	N	L	K	O	L	D	T	E	S	T	A	M	E	N	T	E	L	V	H	I	Q	A	G
O	T	Q	L	M	Z	T	B	A	P	H	H	N	Q	H	G	H	A	P	P	N	C	E	S	H
B	H	X	O	I	H	M	C	G	A	X	C	V	H	B	M	H	H	K	V	C	D	N	X	R
S	Y	U	V	S	C	R	I	P	T	U	R	E	E	E	G	Z	C	Q	Z	K	Z	J	L	J
E	P	T	E	X	N	J	M	E	C	J	C	N	E	W	T	E	S	T	A	M	E	N	T	B
R	Q	P	X	G	M	V	A	S	I	C	R	Q	W	F	T	Z	T	T	R	U	T	H	R	I
V	N	C	J	B	E	N	E	J	W	Q	Z	D	V	D	H	R	Y	I	V	Y	C	O	G	R
A	S	H	P	E	R	S	O	N	A	L	T	R	A	G	A	H	V	N	Q	P	K	X	I	N
T	W	Q	R	F	E	I	X	P	O	W	E	R	F	U	L	Y	Y	S	O	J	H	D	G	O
I	L	D	O	C	T	R	I	N	E	K	G	X	P	X	W	M	X	P	Q	L	V	E	R	A
O	U	T	X	C	O	L	L	E	C	T	I	O	N	M	Y	Q	X	I	Z	Y	T	O	J	N
N	X	C	T	W	E	P	O	T	C	N	L	T	A	W	K	L	I	R	E	B	K	X	X	E
R	Z	C	C	E	A	P	C	R	Q	I	F	Z	I	X	P	C	P	E	T	I	C	G	C	C
M	U	X	H	O	L	Y	S	P	I	R	I	T	X	N	M	V	A	D	S	D	J	J	W	Y
A	S	N	Y	R	D	T	H	P	W	D	M	A	P	P	L	I	C	A	T	I	O	N	P	I

58

We Believe For Kids!

Teacher's Guide

Lesson 5
God the
Father

Lesson 5

Doctrinal Statement:

We believe God is the eternal, all-powerful, all-knowing, every-where-present, and unchangeable Creator of all, who is also the God of love, mercy, and compassion.

Big Question:

Who/what is God?

Lesson Aim:

To introduce students to God the Father.

Key Verse:

"See how very much our Father loves us, for he calls us his children, and that is what we are! But the people who belong to this world don't recognize that we are God's children because they don't know him" (1 John 3:1).

Materials:

A physical Bible for each student
Student's journals

God the Father

Materials: (cont.)

Two copies of the script

Picture of the Mona Lisa or some well-known work of art (on-screen or in a book)

Butcher paper, paintbrush, one or two containers of paint, and a drop cloth

Setup:

Choose two students to act out the script printed in their workbooks [page 137]

Warming Up: [15 minutes]

Review last week's lesson. Pray together as you begin class. Ask that God would give the students understanding.

Skit: [5 minutes]

See the full script on page 173 of the Teacher's Guide and on page 137 of the Student's Journal.

Lesson 5

Going Deeper: [20 minutes]

Today we are going to talk about another father who cares about his children.

Ask a volunteer to read 1 John 3:1.

1 John 3:1:
See how very much our Father loves us, for he calls us his children, and that is what we are! But the people who belong to this world don't recognize that we are God's children because they don't know him.

The Bible tells us in Deuteronomy 6:4 that there is only one God, but He shows himself to us as three persons united in one Godhead (Matthew 28:19). He has shown himself as a:

- **Father** – the Creator of all things (Genesis 1:1)

- **Son** – Jesus, Savior of the whole world (John 3:16) and

- **Helper** – the Holy Spirit, who lives in us and guides us to do what is right (John 14:17 & 26)

Today we will focus on only one of the ways our God has shown Himself to us, a Father.

God the Father

What is a father? *Let students give their responses.*

A father is the male parent of a child or children.

What are some of the duties of a father? *Let students give their responses.*

Yes, a father should protect us, take good care of us, love us, teach us things we need to learn, and help us to grow into better men and women. These are some of the things our earthly fathers should try to do.

God is our Heavenly Father. The Bible states that we are God's children (Romans 8:16). We are God's creation, created for his purpose. That means that God made us for a reason; we were not created by chance (Isaiah 64:8). We are special. God's purpose for each one of us will be revealed as we stay close to Him.

As our earthly father does, God also protects us from harm and danger (Nehemiah 4:20). He cares for us so much that He knows the number of hairs on our heads (Matthew 10:30-31).

Can you count the number of hairs on your head? Let's try.

Grab a small section of your hair and start counting: 1, 2, 3, 4...

I give up! I can't do it!

Lesson 5

Unlike our earthly father, who may leave us or not be available to help us when we are in need, our Heavenly Father, God, will never leave us. God said that when we call, He will answer, and He will be with us always (Psalm 27:10).

Just as we strive to know our earthly fathers better, so we should try to know more about our Heavenly Father.

What can we do to know our Heavenly Father better?

Let students give their responses.

Answers: Read the Bible (God's words to us) daily, obey the Bible, talk to God daily, and attend church services and Sunday school classes

Did you know that we are made in God's image, so we share some of His attributes or qualities? For example, God is good, and we can also be good. God shows mercy when He forgives us for our sins. We can also show mercy when we forgive each other. God loves us, and we also are able to love others. On the count of three, let's shout out the name of someone we love. . . one, two, three . . . (Psalm 100:5 and 116:5).

Although we share some of our Heavenly Father's attributes, there are some qualities He has that are unique to Him

God the Father

alone. We do NOT share these qualities:

God is a spirit. We cannot see Him with our natural eyes. This does not mean that He does not exist. We cannot see gravity or oxygen with our eyes, but that does not mean they do not exist. In fact, some things that you cannot see with your eyes are more vital to your existence than many things you can see.

Ask students to list other examples of things they know exist even though they can't see them.

When we see a magnificent work of art or even something as simple as an old barn, we are aware that someone created it. When you see a video gaming device, even though you do not see its maker, you reason (correctly) that if the gaming device exists, then someone must have made it.

So it is with the universe. We live in a great, big universe. If the universe exists, then someone must have created it; there must be a creator. Our Bible tells us that God is the creator of this great universe. Genesis 1:1 states, "In the beginning God created the heavens and the earth."

The book of Genesis goes on to explain that God also created people. This type of belief is called faith.

Lesson 5

Ask a student to read

Hebrews 11:3:
By faith we understand that the entire universe was formed at God's command, that what we now see did not come from anything that can be seen.

Although God is a spirit without limitations, the Bible speaks of Him in ways we can relate to. The Bible speaks of God's arms and hands (Isaiah 41:10). It also speaks of God's feelings, such as sorrow (Genesis 6:6).

God is omnipotent. This means that He is all powerful; He is the number one ruler of heaven and earth. There is nothing He cannot do (Isaiah 40:28-31).

Close your eyes for a minute and think of the hardest task in the whole world. **Give students a moment to think.**

God can do that thing you are thinking of, and He can do it easily. So never be afraid to ask Him for help. John 15:7 states that "if you are relying totally on God and are obeying his words, you can ask Him for anything and He will do it for you."

God is omniscient. God knows everything. Oh yes, He knows way more than the kids in your classrooms do, even the one that's always raising her hand when the teacher asks a question. He knows the truth about what you did last weekend, even if your parents do not. God is all wise; there is nothing He does not know. He also knows what you have been through (Psalms 139:1-6).

If you are not sure about something, just talk to Him about it and He will make it clearer for you.

God is omnipresent. God is everywhere. He has no limitations. You cannot put God in a box or lock Him in a room. You cannot hide around a corner or behind a door. There is no way you can escape his eyes. God sees everything; nothing takes him by surprise (Psalms 139:7-12).

Always remember that wherever you are, God is with you. So there is no need to feel alone or afraid. The Bible states that He will never leave you or forsake you (Matthew 28:20; Hebrews 13:5).

God is holy. He cannot tolerate sin (1 Peter 1:16). Although we can strive to be holy, we cannot be holy without God.

The crazy thing is our amazing Heavenly Father wants to have a relationship with us (Genesis 1:26; Matthew 23:37). This was His initial plan when He created us, but we sinned, and that sin created a barrier between us and God. Yet He made a way to reconcile us to Himself because He loves us. We will talk more about that next week!

Lesson 5

Activation: [15 minutes]

Show the students the picture of the Mona Lisa (or another work of art). Next have a student dip a paint brush in one of the paint containers and fling it onto the butcher paper. Ask the students if they see an image of a person on the paper. Have the student fling the brush again.

Ask the students:

Do you think that flinging this paintbrush at the paper will ever produce an image as clear as the Mona Lisa?

What about if we spilled the paint can? Do you think over time, if we kept spilling the paint, that we would produce an image of a person?

When you see the Mona Lisa, do you think, "What a happy accident?" Or do you think, "Wow, an artist must have planned and created this work of art?"

Ask the students to notice God's creation in the world around us as well as items created by people.

Ask them to name specific items. Then ask, What do the "creations" tell us about their creators?

Closing: [10 minutes]

Journal Activity

Discuss the following questions:

How are we like God?

How are we different from God?

Did you learn something in this lesson about God that surprised you? If so, what?

How does it make you feel to know that God knows what you are doing every minute of the day?

Were you surprised to learn that God wants a relationship with you?

Close in prayer.

We Believe For Kids!

Teacher's Guide

Lesson 6
God the
Son

Lesson 6

Doctrinal Statement:

We believe Jesus is co-Creator with the Father. Conceived miraculously, He is all human and all God. He died and rose again to make possible our relationship with God. Now He is in heaven with the Father praying for us.

Big Question:

Who is Jesus Christ?

Lesson Aim:

To introduce students to Jesus Christ.

Key Verse:

"But God showed his great love for us by sending Christ to die for us while we were still sinners" (Romans 5:8).

Materials:

A physical Bible for each student
Student's journals
Tape
Scissors

God the Son

Warming Up: [15 minutes]

Welcome the students and open in prayer. Pray that students will realize the significance of Jesus' death and resurrection.

God has shown himself to us in three different ways: God the Father, God the Son, and God the Holy Spirit. These three roles are equal in power and work together in accomplishing the great task that God has set out to do: restore the relationship between humankind and Himself.

Last week we focused on God the Father and Creator of the universe. Today we will focus on God the Son, but first let me tell you a true story about a widow and her son

Lesson 6

Story:

Once there was a poor widow who lived in a small village in a faraway country. She had a son named Ajouni but everyone called him AJ.

AJ was a good-hearted child, but he was a bit headstrong, and often got himself into trouble. His antics would usually end up costing his mother greatly – in the time and money it took for her to fix whatever mess AJ had gotten himself into and in the heartache she felt worrying about him. This would frustrate AJ's mother immensely, but she determined that she would never give up on her son. The widow worked long, hard hours to earn money any way she could and skimped on her own clothing and food. She wanted to make sure AJ had all the opportunities other children had.

When AJ reached tenth grade, he decided schoolwork wasn't important. So, even though he led his mom to believe that he was leaving the house to attend school each day, he would instead go to the video arcade. He did this for several months.

Finally, it was time for the tenth graders to move on to the eleventh grade. The widow was so excited. Her dreams of seeing AJ finishing school and moving on to a bright future were coming to pass!

God the Son

But when she went to AJ's school to sign the necessary papers for him to move up a grade, she received devastating news. The principal told AJ's mom that not only was he not going to advance to eleventh grade, but he had also been expelled! He had missed too many days of school and had failed to complete the requirements.

The poor widow was angry, disappointed, and heartbroken. Now AJ's chances for a better life were ruined. All her sacrifice had gone to waste! Angrily, she told her son, "AJ, I worked so hard to send you to school and this is how you show your gratitude?!"

For the first time, the poor woman felt like giving up on her son, and AJ could sense her frustration. He stopped and took a hard look at his mother. Her labors had taken a toll. She looked much older than the other women her age. Deep wrinkles were etched into her face. She walked with a slight stoop, having carried loads much too heavy for her stature, and her hands were gnarled and rough. For the first time in his life, AJ felt remorse as he realized how much his carefree lifestyle had affected his mom. That night he could not sleep. His mother had every right to put him out of the house.

The next day, however, the widow announced, "AJ, I have a plan to help you reach success, but this is your last chance."

She took all the money she had – every single dollar – and visited several schools, hoping someone would give AJ a second chance. When she had nearly run out of options and hope, she found a school that would accept him on a trial basis.

Appreciating how much his mother had sacrificed for him, AJ studied hard, ignoring his friends' constant invitations to party. His efforts paid off, and he graduated with honors. His teachers went on to describe him as "well-mannered and extremely smart." On graduation day the widow was all smiles. She was so glad she didn't give up on her son.

Main Story points

As we go through this lesson, keep in mind the following story points.

- **The widow did not give up on her son.**
- **The widow envisioned a good outcome for her son.**
- **The widow devised a plan to get her son back on track when he messed up.**

God the Son

Going Deeper: [20 minutes]

Ask the students, Who is a daughter? *Let students respond.*

Yes, a daughter is any female child. The sisters, female classmates, mothers, aunts and other female individuals in our lives are someone's daughter.

Ask the students, Who is a son? *Let students respond.*

Yes, a son is any male child. Our brothers, fathers, uncles, and other male individuals in our lives – all of them are someone's son.

Jesus Christ is also someone's son. He is the son of God and Mary *(Matthew 1:18).*

He was born to an earthly mother, which makes Him fully human and He was born to a Heavenly Father, which makes Him fully God.

What does this really mean?

This means that Jesus Christ is fully human just like us, but unlike us, He is fully God.

How can this be?

It's a bit hard to comprehend. But remember: God is all powerful. God, in His great power, sent Himself as Jesus Christ to earth.

Lesson 6

Ask students to look up the following verses:

John 1:1
In the beginning the Word already existed. The Word was with God, and the Word was God.

And John 1:14
So the Word became human and made his home among us.

God and his word cannot be separated; they are one and the same. So, to say the word became flesh and made his home among us is to say God himself came in human form to live with us. Isn't that awesome?

Jesus told us in Scripture that He and the Father are the same. No, they are not twins or clones of each other. They are the same person fulfilling different roles *(John 14:9-10)*.

For example, your father plays the role of dad to you; he also plays the role of a son to his parents.

You see, Jesus, the Son of God, came in human form so that He could fully relate to us. He wanted to feel the things we feel – things like pain, temptation, joy, sadness, and conflict.

Jesus becoming human enabled us to see what God is like; it helped us to relate to Him. And He became the perfect role model for how we should act. He showed us that we have the ability to overcome things that Jesus overcame. He was tempted, lied to, neglected, and rejected, but He overcame it all in his human state. Now, through the strength He gives us, we can do all things *(Philippians 4:13)*.

So, why did our Heavenly Father send Jesus Christ to earth?

Let's look back at the story of the widow and her son. The widow had a plan for her son. She wanted him to succeed in life. She saw a bright future for him. Similarly, God has a plan for us *(Jeremiah 29:11)*.

God's plan is to give us a hopeful future. To have hope is to look forward to something. So, God's plan is to give us a future we can look forward to. But like the widow whose son had messed up, Adam and Eve sinned in the Garden of Eden when they disobeyed God. A sin nature, our natural desire to do what is wrong, was then passed down from them into all humans born thereafter *(Romans 3:23)*. That is why we are tempted to lie, steal, cheat, or disobey our parents.

This was not what God intended. God's original plan was to have a close relationship with us. He made us in his image and gave us power over all things, but Adam and Eve's sin created a distance between us and God. In other words, sin separated us from God.

God wanted to bring us back to Him, to remove the distance between us, but there was a price that had to be paid, kind of similar to paying a fine. Only this fine was very costly. God needed to find a perfect person who had not sinned to pay the price for our sins by giving His life. The Bible states that the wages for sin is death *(Romans 6:23)*. (Our wages on earth are the payment we earn for working. The wages of sin are the payment we earned for our sins.)

Therefore, if someone did not die for us, we would have to die for our own sins, that's how bad sin is. However, this death does not refer simply to physical death, like when our loved ones pass away.

This death refers to being separated from God forever. Isn't that sad?

God the Son

God looked everywhere but there was no one who was sinless –
not one person *(Psalm 53:2-3; Romans 3:10-12)*.

So, like the widow, God made a plan that involved a huge sacrifice.
He sent what He treasured most, His only Son, to earth in human
form to pay the price for our sins. Jesus Christ, God's Son, was
crucified on the cross for our sins. Even though He was tempted,
beaten, and killed He remained sinless. Christ later rose from
the dead and ascended to heaven. He defeated sin and death, and
removed the distance between people and God. Now we can have
a relationship with God our Father through his Son, Jesus Christ.

Lesson 6

This was God's plan, to give us a second chance, to restore our relationship with him, to get us back on track *(John 17:3-4)*.

> *John 3:16*
> *For this is how God loved the world: He gave his one and only Son, so that everyone who believes in him, will not perish but have eternal life.*

So, everyone who believes in Jesus Christ, who died on the cross for our sins and rose from the dead, shall be saved. But first we need to ask God to forgive us for all the wrong things we have done and turn away from doing wrong. His ultimate desire for us is to have an amazing future, to enjoy eternal life with Him.

Now, when God, our Heavenly Father, sees us He sees the righteousness of his Son, Jesus Christ. This means that we are now in right standing with God but only through Jesus Christ.

Remember, not everyone is in right standing with God. Only those who have accepted Jesus Christ into their hearts, believe in Him, and have turned away from their sinful ways.

Galatians 3:22 states that we are all prisoners of sin; it traps us. We receive God's promise of freedom only by believing in Jesus Christ.

We will discuss this more in chapter 17: Sin/Salvation.

God the Son

Activation: [15 minutes]

The following activities will be in the student workbooks as well. Allow the students to work on them as time allows.

Activity 1

Unscramble the verse below:

JESSU EVAG SHI ILFE FRO URO SNIS, TUSJ SA DGO URO HERTAF PLNNAED, NI RDERO OT ESRUEC SU MROF ISHT LIVE WLDOR NI WCIHH EW ILVE.

[Answer: Galatians 1:4 NLT]

Activity 2

On page 56 in your Student Journal, draw a line from each characteristic that we share with God to the figure of the person and draw a line from each characteristic that is unique to God to the word "God".

Activity 3 [do as a class]

Jesus, The Son of God Bible Challenge

Place students into two groups. It can be girls against boys or an even split in numbers. Choose two students (or youth staff) to serve as judges that will determine whose hand goes up first. The teacher or other youth staff will read off a question. Team members are not allowed to shout out their answers to the questions, but must raise their hand instead. Whichever student raises their hand first gets the first chance to answer the question. If the answer is correct that team is awarded a point. If a student shouts out the answer without waiting to be recognized, his or her team will not be awarded a point. Teachers can adapt this game to fit their students' needs.

Part 1: Questions: True or False

1. **Jesus is the son of Adam**

2. **Jesus was born to an earthly father.**

3. **Jesus was fully God.**

4. **Sin does not affect our relationship with God.**

5. **We were all born into sin.**

6. **Jesus is fully man.**

Part 2: Questions

1. **Why did Jesus come to earth? (4 points)**

2. **What was God's final plan for us? (2 points)**

3. **What do we mean when we say not everyone is in right standing with God? Does that mean some people are better than others? (4 points)**

4. **Quote by heart this week's key verse. (6 points)**

Closing: [10 minutes]

Ask the following questions:

Do you believe in Jesus Christ?

Do you believe that He died on the cross for your sins and rose again?

Have you asked Him to forgive you for the wrong things you have done?

Are you willing to turn away from doing what is wrong?

Lesson 6

If your answers were YES, then pray with me.

Lead the children in a prayer, such as the following:

Dear Heavenly Father,

You paid a huge price for my sins by sending your Son to die on the cross for me. Thank you for doing that! When I think about my life, I realize that I have done things and thought about things that are wrong, and I am sorry. Please forgive me. Please replace my sinful nature, my desire to do and think wrong things, with your nature, with your Holy Spirit instead. Help me to do the things that make You happy.

In Jesus' name I pray, amen.

If you prayed this prayer with me, congratulations! You now have a relationship with Jesus, God's Son! You can talk with Him anytime you want. Please let me know about your decision so I can be praying with you!

Close in another prayer praying for students who began a new relationship with Jesus, that God will help them follow Him and to grow in their relationship with Him.

We Believe For Kids!

Teacher's Guide

Lesson 7
God the
Holy Spirit

Lesson 7

Doctrinal Statement:

We believe in God the Holy Spirit, co-Creator with the Father and the Son. He helps us know when we've done wrong, make good decisions, and learn what is true. He gives us power and the tools to be like Jesus.

Big Question:

Who is the Holy Spirit?

Lesson Aim:

To introduce students to the Holy Spirit.

Key Verse:

"And I will ask the Father, and he will give you another Advocate, who will never leave you" (John 14:16).

Materials:

A physical Bible for each student
Student's journals
Essential oil, such as lavender oil

God the Holy Spirit

Materials: (cont)

Diffuser
White board and marker or butcher paper

Setup:

Gather materials.

Pray for your students during the week and ask the Holy Spirit to show them His presence.

Warming Up: [15 minutes]

Welcome the students and open with prayer. Recap last week's lesson.

Remember, there is only one God. He has shown himself to us as three persons, and in three different ways: God the Father, God the Son, and God the Holy Spirit. All these roles are equal in power and work together in the completion of God's divine plan for us.

Lesson 7

Today we will focus on God the Holy Spirit. The Holy Spirit is sometimes called a helper. In the New American Standard Version of the Bible, our key verse reads like this: "I will ask the Father, and He will give you another Helper, that He may be with you forever."

In this passage, Jesus is telling his disciples that He would pray to God the Father, that He would give them a helper, someone to be with them always as He had been. Jesus was leaving earth and did not want the disciples to feel alone. So, as He ascended to heaven, God sent his own Spirit, the Holy Spirit, to live in the hearts of his disciples and all who believed in Jesus Christ.

When we accept Jesus Christ as our Savior, his Spirit comes and lives inside our hearts. His Spirit is our Helper.

When you hear the word helper, what comes to your mind?
Let the students answer.

Yes, simply put, a helper is one who helps.

God the Holy Spirit

Story:

When Saira was a little girl, her mom and dad traveled often, so they brought a lady to their home to live with Saira and her four sisters. The girls asked their mom if the lady was a relative, but their mom replied, "No, she is your helper."

For a minute the girls were excited. "A helper," they thought. "Cool! Maybe our helper will wash the dishes and do all the chores for us!" This would certainly give them more time to play, right? But they were so wrong.

Maureen, the helper, did help the girls to do many things but they still had to do their share of the work. Sometimes Maureen would do some of the chores by herself, but usually she would take the time to teach the girls how to do their chores on their own. She taught them things like making their beds properly, cooking a quick meal, making good choices, and many other things that made them better able to take care of themselves.

Maureen was a great helper. When the girls made mistakes, she would help them to clean up the mess before their mother came home. She also showed the girls how to avoid making the same mistakes over again. Soon the girls thought of Maureen as part of the family. Just as their parents did, Maureen made the girls feel safe. They knew they could depend on her help.

Going Deeper: [25 minutes]
Getting to Know Our Helper.

Like God the Father and God the Son, the Holy Spirit is also fully God. God is a spirit and He cannot be limited. As you have seen from our previous lessons, He can show himself to us in different ways. Therefore, the Holy Spirit is God in spirit form, living inside of us.

Ask one of the students to read Romans 8:11, emphasizing how powerful He is, that He raised Jesus from the dead!

This verse ways that "The Spirit of God, who raised Jesus from the dead, lives in you." So ask yourself, "If God's Spirit lives inside of me, should I be afraid?

No! We should never be afraid because we have the powerful Holy Spirit living inside of us. Whenever you feel afraid, remind yourself of who's inside of you.

Why did God send the Holy Spirit?

The Holy Spirit was sent by God to carry out His will in and through us. He is at work in our hearts to make us better children of God. For example, that weird feeling we get when we are doing something wrong is the Holy Spirit's way of showing us that what we are doing is not right.

God the Holy Spirit

So, when we are disobedient or disrespectful to our parents, we often feel guilty afterward. But as soon as we obey that urge to apologize, we feel much better. That's the Holy Spirit at work in us, helping us to do what's right.

The Holy Spirit will also try to prevent us from doing what is wrong in the first place. For example, sometimes we are tempted to make a poor choice and the Holy Spirit shows us a better option. We should listen to this voice because this is the Holy Spirit trying to spare us from suffering the consequences of a bad decision.

Making the choice to do what is right can still be difficult, but the Spirit of God inside of us gives us the power to make the right choice. Isn't that wonderful?

Here are some other ways the Holy Spirit helps us:

Have students look up the following passages and be ready to read them at the right time (Romans 8:26; Colossians 1:8; Ephesians 1:17). At the top of a white board or butcher paper, write down the ways the Holy Spirit helps us.

The students should write them in their books as well. Then ask the students to think of an example of each of these situations. If there is time, they could share the examples with the class. You may need to give them an example at first to get them started.

Romans 8:26 states that the Holy Spirit prays for us and helps us with our weaknesses. So if you have a weakness such as lying, jealousy, or selfishness and you are trying really hard to do better, the Holy Spirit doesn't just say NMP (not my problem). No, the Holy Spirit talks to God on your behalf and helps you to overcome your weaknesses. The Holy Spirit prays for us!

Have you ever had a time where the Holy Spirit has helped you with a weakness? I know I have. **Share an example.**

Colossians 1:8 tells us that the Holy Spirit helps us to love others. So when you see those people that give you a hard time and you silently say to yourself, "I don't like him or her," the Holy Spirit can give you more understanding and compassion for them. He can help you love those individuals because God wants all of us to love each other. The Holy Spirit helps us to love others.

Has anyone here ever had the Holy Spirit help you be able to be kind to someone you didn't like at first? **Let students answer.**

Ephesians 1:17 states that the Holy Spirit will help us understand God better. The Holy Spirit makes the Bible clearer to us as we read it. Sometimes when we come across others who are hurting, the Holy Spirit will bring the specific word of God that they need to our minds so we can offer comfort and encouragement.

This is why we need to read the word of God daily.

God the Holy Spirit

Have you ever been trying to help someone who was having a hard time and you felt like the Lord gave you the words to say to them?

We can relate to the Holy Spirit as a person, not a thing, because the Holy Spirit can teach, pray, love, and feel sadness just like we do. Isaiah 63:10 tells us that when we rebel against God or reject His ways and choose to do what is wrong, we grieve the Holy Spirit. Yes, the Holy Spirit can feel sorrow.

The Complete Picture

When we allow the Spirit of God to guide us, we are more likely to please God. The more we allow the Holy Spirit to lead us, the more the fruit of the Spirit will show in our daily lives and we will become more and more like Jesus.

The Bible states that the Holy Spirit produces good qualities, or "fruit," in our lives: love, joy, peace, patience, kindness, goodness, faithfulness, gentleness, and self-control (Galatians 5:22-23).

Okay, close your eyes and imagine you have a friend with all these qualities. Wouldn't it be nice to be around them?

Now, imagine yourself with all the fruit of the Spirit. Let's say them again: *love, joy, peace, patience, kindness, goodness, faithfulness, gentleness, and self-control.*

Lesson 7

The Holy Spirit can give you these qualities if you allow Him to lead you by obeying Him as He nudges you to do the things that please God.

The Holy Spirit is an amazing helper. Besides helping us do the right things, the Holy Spirit also gives us the power to serve others and tell them about God. We will talk about that more in a later lesson. The Holy Spirit does the will of God and makes us better, from the inside out. He makes us act more like Jesus!

God the Holy Spirit

Activation: [10 minutes]

Oil was often used in the Bible to represent the Holy Spirit. I am going to place some scented oil in this diffuser to illustrate one of the powerful functions of the Holy Spirit.

Ask the students if they can tell which fragrance you used. Give them time to answer.

Yes, you knew I used lavender (or whatever fragrance used) oil because of its fragrance. The Holy Spirit carries a "fragrance" with Him as well. He carries God's fragrance. When we ask the Holy Spirit to direct our lives it's as if we become a "diffuser" for Him. Just as the lavender oil makes this room take on the characteristic fragrance of lavender, the Holy Spirit wants to help us take on the "fragrance," or characteristics of God. We talked about some of those characteristics in our lesson; we called them "fruits of the Spirit." Can you name them?

Answer: love, joy, peace, patience, kindness, goodness, faithfulness, gentleness, and self-control

Allow students time to complete the journaling activities in their journals.

Lesson 7

Closing: [10 minutes]

The Holy Spirit can help us see areas in our lives that are not pleasing to God – in our attitudes and in our actions. It's kind of like running a virus scan on our computer or phone that reveals where the trouble spots are. The Holy Spirit speaks in different ways, but often He speaks to us through thoughts He gives us. Let's pray and thank God for the Holy Spirit. Ask the Holy Spirit to show you areas in your life that do not please God and then ask Him to help you in those areas. Then ask Him to show you ways you do please Him.

Take time to let the students reflect. Maybe play some soft music in the background.

Encourage the students to find ways the Holy Spirit helps them throughout the day and to listen carefully for ways He is guiding them.

Close in prayer.

We Believe For Kids!

Teacher's Guide

Lesson 8
Review

Lesson 8

Doctrinal Statements:

- We believe God is the eternal, all-powerful, all-knowing, every-where-present, and unchangeable Creator of all, who is also the God of love, mercy, and compassion.

- We believe Jesus is co-Creator with the Father. Conceived miraculously, He is all human and all God. He died and rose again to make possible our relationship with God. Now He is in heaven with the Father praying for us.

- We believe in God the Holy Spirit, co-Creator with the Father and the Son. He helps us know when we've done wrong, make good decisions, and learn what is true. He gives us power and the tools to be like Jesus.

Review Big Questions:

Who/what is God?

Who is Jesus Christ?

Who is the Holy Spirit?

Review

Lesson Aim:

Review lessons 5, 6, and 7 on God the Father, God the Son, and God the Holy Spirit

Materials:

A physical Bible for each student
Student's journals

Lesson 8

Review Lesson 5: God the Father

Doctrinal Statement:

We believe God is the eternal, all-powerful, all-knowing, everywhere-present, and unchangeable Creator of all, who is also the God of love, mercy, and compassion.

Key Verse:

1 John 3:1
See how very much our Father loves us, for he calls us his children, and that is what we are! But the people who belong to this world don't recognize that we are God's children because they don't know him.

Main Points:

- The Bible tells us in Deuteronomy 6:4 that there is only one God, but He shows himself to us as three persons united in one Godhead *(Matthew 28:19)*.

- God is our Heavenly Father. The Bible states that we are God's children *(Romans 8:16)*. We are God's creation, created for his purpose. That means that God made us for a reason; we were not created by chance *(Isaiah 64:8)*. We are special. God's purpose for each one of us will be revealed as we stay close to Him.

Review

- We are made in God's image, so we share some of His attributes or qualities? For example, God is good, and we can also be good. God shows mercy when He forgives us for our sins. We can also show mercy when we forgive each other. God loves us, and we also are able to love others.

- Although we share some of our Heavenly Father's attributes, there are some qualities He has that are unique to Him alone. We do NOT share these qualities:

    - **God is a spirit.** We cannot see Him with our natural eyes.

    - **God is omnipotent.** This means that He is all powerful; He is the number one ruler of heaven and earth. There is nothing He cannot do *(Isaiah 40:28-31)*.

    - **God is omniscient.** God knows everything. God is all wise; there is nothing He does not know. He also knows what you have been through *(Psalms 139:1-6)*.

    - **God is omnipresent.** God is everywhere. He has no limitations. You cannot put God in a box or lock Him in a room. You cannot hide around a corner or behind a door. There is no way you can escape his eyes. God sees everything; nothing takes Him by surprise *(Psalms 139:7-12)*.

    - **God is holy.** He cannot tolerate sin *(1 Peter 1:16)*. Although we can strive to be holy, we cannot be holy without God.

Review Lesson 6: God the Son

Doctrinal Statement:

We believe Jesus is co-Creator with the Father. Conceived miraculously, He is all human and all God. He died and rose again to make possible our relationship with God. Now He is in heaven with the Father praying for us.

Key Verse:

Romans 5:8
But God showed his great love for us by sending Christ to die for us while we were still sinners.

Main Points:

- Jesus Christ is someone's son. He is the son of God and Mary (Matthew 1:18).

- He was born to an earthly mother, which makes Him fully human and He was born to a Heavenly Father, which makes Him fully God.

- God and his word cannot be separated; they are one and the same. So, to say the Word became flesh and made his home among us is to say God himself came in human form to live with us (John 1:1; 1:14).

Review

- Jesus told us in Scripture that He and the Father are the same. They are the same person fulfilling different roles *(John 14:9-10)*.

- Jesus becoming human enabled us to see what God is like; it helped us to relate to Him. And He became the perfect role model for how we should act. He showed us that we have the ability to overcome things that Jesus overcame. He was tempted, lied to, neglected, and rejected, but He overcame it all in his human state. Now, through the strength He gives us, we can do all things *(Philippians 4:13)*.

- A sin nature, our natural desire to do what is wrong, was passed down from Adam and Eve into all humans born thereafter *(Romans 3:23)*. This was not what God intended. God's original plan was to have a close relationship with us. He made us in his image and gave us power over all things, but Adam and Eve's sin created a distance between us and God. In other words, sin separated us from God.

- God wanted to bring us back to Him, to remove the distance between us, but there was a price that had to be paid. God needed to find a perfect person who had not sinned to pay the price for our sins by giving His life. The Bible states that the wages for sin is death *(Romans 6:23)*.

- God looked everywhere but there was no one who was sinless – not one person *(Psalm 53:2-3; Romans 3:10-12)*. God made a plan that involved a huge sacrifice. He sent what He treasured most, His only Son, to earth in human form to pay the price for our sins. Jesus Christ, God's Son, was crucified on the cross for our sins. Even though He was tempted, beaten, and killed He remained sinless. Christ later rose from the dead and ascended to heaven. He defeated sin and death, and removed the distance between people and God. Now we can have a relationship with God our Father through his Son, Jesus Christ.

- Everyone who believes in Jesus Christ, who died on the cross for our sins and rose from the dead, shall be saved. But first we need to ask God to forgive us for all the wrong things we have done and turn away from doing wrong. His ultimate desire for us is to have an amazing future, to enjoy eternal life with Him.

- Now, when God, our Heavenly Father, sees us He sees the righteousness of his Son, Jesus Christ. This means that we are now in right standing with God but only through Jesus Christ.

Review

Review Lesson 7: God the Holy Spirit

Doctrinal Statement:

We believe in God the Holy Spirit, co-Creator with the Father and the Son. He helps us know when we've done wrong, make good decisions, and learn what is true. He gives us power and the tools to be like Jesus.

Key Verse:

John 14:16
And I will ask the Father, and he will give you another Advocate, who will never leave you.

Main Points:

- When we accept Jesus Christ as our Savior, his Spirit comes and lives inside our hearts. His Spirit is our Helper.

- Like God the Father and God the Son, the Holy Spirit is also fully God. God is a spirit and He cannot be limited. As you have seen from our previous lessons, He can show himself to us in different ways. Therefore, the Holy Spirit is God in spirit form, living inside of us.

- The Holy Spirit was sent by God to carry out His will in and through us. He is at work in our hearts to make us better children of God.

Lesson 8

- The Holy Spirit will also try to prevent us doing what is wrong.

- The Holy Spirit prays for us and helps us with our weaknesses. The Holy Spirit talks to God on your behalf and helps you to overcome your weaknesses *(Romans 8:26)*.

- The Holy Spirit helps us to love others *(Colossians 1:8)*.

- The Holy Spirit will help us understand God better. The Holy Spirit makes the Bible clearer to us as we read it. Sometimes when we come across others who are hurting, the Holy Spirit will bring the specific word of God that they need to our minds so we can offer comfort and encouragement *(Ephesians 1:17)*.

- We can relate to the Holy Spirit as a person, not a thing, because the Holy Spirit can teach, pray, love, and feel sadness just like we do. *Isaiah 63:10* tells us that when we rebel against God or reject His ways and choose to do what is wrong, we grieve the Holy Spirit. Yes, the Holy Spirit can feel sorrow.

- The Bible states that the Holy Spirit produces good qualities, or "fruit," in our lives: love, joy, peace, patience, kindness, goodness, faithfulness, gentleness, and self-control *(Galatians 5:22-23)*.

Review

Review Questions:

These are the answers to the review questions in the Student's Journal.

1. God shows Himself to us as **three** persons united in one Godhead *(Matthew 28:19)*.

2. The three persons of the Godhead are: God the **Father**, God the **Son**, and God the Holy **Spirit**.

3. We are made in God's image so we share some of His attributes or qualites. Which of the following do we share with God?

4. a. omnipotence, omniscience, omnipresence, holiness
   b. **goodness**, **mercifulness**, **love**
   c. eyes, legs, hands

5. **Omnipotent** means that God is all powerful.

6. **Omniscient** means that God is all knowing.

7. **Omnipresent** means that God is everywhere.

8. Since Jesus was born to an earthly mother, he is fully **human**.

9. Since Jesus was born to a Heavenly Father, he is fully **God**.

10. We can know what the Father is like buy knowing **Jesus** (the Son).

11. Our natural desire to do what is wrong is called a **sin** nature.

12. Our sin **seperates** us from God.

13. By his death and ressurection, Jesus paid the **price** for our sin.

14. The Holy Spirit is our **helper**.

15. The Holy Spirit does which of the following for us:
    a. Works in our hearts to make us better children of God
    b. Tries to prevent us from doing what is wrong.
    c. Prays for us.
    d. Helps us to love others
    e. Helps us to understand God better.
    f. **All of the above**

16. The Holy Spirit produces good "**fruit**" in our lives: love, joy, peace, patience, kindness, goodness, faithfulness, gentleness, and self-control *(Galatians 5:22-23)*.

Review

Crossword:

The answers to the crossword will be the same as the Review Questions.

Crossword Answers:

Down:

1. the Holy Spirit is this to us

2. all powerful

3. the Holy Spirit produces this in us

4. everywhere

5. part of the Godhead

7. what our sin does between us and God

10. born of an earthly mother

12. born of a Heavenly Father

13. natural desire to do wrong

15. part of the Godhead

Across:

6. the Son

8. paid for by Jesus

9. part of the Godhead

11. number of persons united in one Godhead

14. all knowing

We Believe For Kids!

Teacher's Guide

Lesson 9
God
Speaks

Lesson 9

Doctrinal Statement:

We believe that even though God is the eternal, all-powerful, all-knowing, everywhere-present, and unchangeable Creator of all, He wants a relationship with each one of us.

Big Question:

How does God communicate with us?

Lesson Aim:

To convince students that God wants to and does speak to each of us, and we are able to hear His voice.

Key Verse:

"My sheep listen to my voice; I know them, and they follow me" (John 10:27).

Materials:

Bibles for each student
Student's journals
Pencils
Highlighters

God Speaks

Materials: (cont)

White board or butcher paper

Setup:

Pray for your students this week, that they will begin to hear God speaking to them.

You may want to print the scriptures about children who heard from God on separate strips of paper to hand to each group. (Scriptures are in the "Going Deeper" section.)

Warming Up: [15 minutes]

Open in prayer. Hopefully by now some students are comfortable praying aloud. If so, ask for a volunteer to lead the class in praying over your time together. If not, pray over the time yourself, asking that each student would hear God speak to them in a personal way today.

Ask for volunteers to look up and mark the following verses in their Bibles to read aloud later: John 8:47, John 10:27, Jeremiah 33:3, and Deuteronomy 30:14.

Lesson 9

Read the doctrinal statement together. Discuss as a group what it means that God wants a relationship or a friendship with us.

What do healthy friendships look like? Do good friends mostly talk, or do they listen as well?

Guide the discussion to establish the truth that communication in good relationships goes both ways. In our friendship with God, we get to talk to Him in prayer, but we also get to listen.

To say that we need to be listening to God means that we believe He speaks to us. Do you believe that?

Give kids time to think and answer.

What ways does He speak, either in the Bible or to people today? In what ways has He spoken to you?

As kids answer, make a visible list on the whiteboard or butcher paper. Supplement the kids' list with some of *these answers, defining and discussing them as you go:*

- *Audible "out loud" voice*
- *Inner voice*
- *Sudden thought/idea*
- *Feeling/Impression*
- *Scripture*
- *Words from others*
- *Signs*
- *Dreams*
- *Mental Pictures*
- *Art and music*

Going Deeper: [15 minutes]

There are so many examples in the Bible of people who heard from God. I've got a list here of a few of them, but there's something special about this list. Every person on my list began hearing from God when he or she was a child. Actually, a lot of them were right around your age when they first heard his voice.

God doesn't just speak to adults; He also speaks to kids. Jesus told his disciples that his entire kingdom belongs to kids *(Luke 18:16)*, so there's nothing in his kingdom that doesn't include you. His gifts, his voice, his Word, his Holy Spirit — God wants you to experience all of it!

Lesson 9

Divide the kids into groups of 2-3. Give each group one person from the list below of kids in the Bible who heard from God, along with the accompanying Scripture reference.

Choose someone in your group to read your passage and decide together in what ways God spoke to that person. Be prepared to assist kids in looking up the references, but encourage them to come up with their answers on their own. Afterwards, allow time for kids to share their answers and discuss.

- *I Samuel 3:1-10 (Samuel hearing God)*
- *Psalm 40:3 (David hearing God)*
- *Genesis 37:5-11 (Joseph hearing God)*
- *Daniel 7:1 (Daniel hearing God)*
- *Luke 1:26, 46-55 (Mary hearing God)*

Share with the kids some additional information about each person.

- Samuel heard God when he was 12 years old.
- Many believe David began playing and writing music as young as his teenage years.
- Joseph was about 17 when he had his first dreams.

God Speaks

- Daniel could have been as young as 8 years old when he was taken to Babylon and began hearing God.

- Many believe Mary was around 13 years old when she was first visited by the angel.

Did You Know?

Even though its ears are extremely simple, a moth can sense frequencies up to 300 kilohertz, well beyond the range of any other animal and higher than any bat can squeak.

Did You Know?

Elephants have some of the best hearing around. They can hear at frequencies 20 times lower than humans. It isn't just their ears that perceive sound; these majestic beasts also have receptors in their trunks and feet that are excellent at picking up low-frequency vibrations.

Lesson 9

The stories in the Bible of these kids' lives give us biblical evidence that God spoke not only to adults, but also to kids. But what about now? Does He still speak? **Let students discuss.**

I want to look at a few Scriptures together that say God does still speak to us, and that we are able to hear Him. **Have the kids who marked the verses in their Bibles earlier read their verses, one at a time, pausing after each to discuss the meaning.**

John 8:47:
Anyone who belongs to God listens gladly to the words of God.

John 10:27:
My sheep listen to my voice; I know them, and they follow me.

Jeremiah 33:3:
Ask me and I will tell you remarkable secrets you do not know about things to come.

Deuteronomy 30:14:
No, the message is very close at hand; it is on your lips and in your heart so that you can obey it.

God Speaks

We talked a few weeks ago about how God's Word is living and active. That means that the words we just read are still true today. God is still wanting to speak to you today. In fact, He is speaking to you all the time. It just takes practice to learn to know when the voice we're hearing is His voice.

So, how do we know when it's Him? Let's remember what we learned about God's Word from our first few lessons together. His Word is living and active, but what other characteristics does it have?

Allow kids to brainstorm, prompting them with the first few characteristics from the list below.

Gods Words are:

powerful, transformative, sweet, perfect, true, enlightening, helpful, kind, lovely, etc.

Anything we hear from God's voice is going to fall into these categories. If we don't feel better or cleaner or more free after hearing it, it's not God. Even his corrections are sweet, and lead us toward freedom and joy. He will never lie to you, be cruel to you, or hurt you in any way.

One of the trickiest things to learn is how to tell the difference between God's voice and other voices that influence our lives.

Lesson 9

The three most common voices we hear are: God's voice, Satan's voice, and our own voice. We've talked about God's voice already. What are some characteristics of Satan's voice and our own voice?

Satan's voice:

Satan is our enemy. Scripture says he's a deceiver and an accuser, so when he speaks he will try to lie, trick, confuse, anger, blame, or scare you. If you're hearing something that makes you feel those emotions, it's often Satan who is behind it.

Our own voice:

Our voice speaks to us about our own wants and desires. It's interested in our comfort and is pretty self-serving. If our thoughts are consumed with what's best for us and what we want or wish, odds are it's our own voice speaking to us.

As an example, let's say you're at school and you see Nadia, a girl who recently moved from Russia to your community. Nadia doesn't speak very good English yet and hasn't made many friends. One day, you see a group of popular kids making fun of Nadia's accent, saying rude things to her in English and laughing when she can't understand them. Your gut instinct is to go over there and sit with her, telling the other kids to quit being mean. Almost immediately, though, you begin to think, "Wait, if I go over there, those kids will start being mean to me.

God Speaks

They're popular and I'll probably ruin my chances of being friends with them." After that thought, you begin to hear thoughts like, "I'm such a jerk. I'm nothing but a coward who's too weak and scared to go stick up for someone. No one should want to be my friend. I'm not even a good person."

Whose voice did you hear first? **Let students respond.**

Yes, the first voice or instinct you had was from God, because He cares for the hurting and encourages others. Who did you hear second? **Let students respond.**

Right, the second voice was pretty self-focused, so it was probably your own voice. And whose voice did you hear last? **Let students respond.**

Yep, that was likely Satan's voice. He was accusing you, lying to you, and making you feel terrible about who you are.

It can be hard at first to discern the difference between these three. But just like in any friendship, you begin to know God's voice the more you talk with and listen to Him. Just like you would be able to recognize your best friend's voice in a crowd of people, you'll soon be able to pick out God's voice in the midst of a noisy crowd.

Lesson 9

Activation: [15 minutes]

We're going to take a few minutes and practice this. In your journals, you'll see a page that has three headings: **God's Voice, Satan's Voice, and My Voice.** I want you to take a moment to think about some things God's voice says about you, or says to you. What is He speaking to you this morning? Jot down one to three things you hear (or as many as you want!).

Next, take a moment to think of some of the things you tell yourself often. These might be positive or negative. How do you feel about yourself? How do you feel about your life, your family, your friends? What are some of your core wants and desires that you think about often? Jot down a few of those.

Finally, what are some things you suspect Satan says to you? What are some major fears you struggle with, ugly feelings you have toward yourself or others, or lies he may be trying to tell you?

This is a private activity and you don't have to share this with anyone unless you want to. It's important to realize that Satan lies to all of us, and we also all have selfish desires and motivations sometimes. None of us should feel ashamed of what we write down.

Instead, we get an incredible opportunity to reject the selfish or untrue things in the last two categories and fully take in all that God is speaking to us. It might help if when you're done you cross out the lies in Satan's category, as well as anything that isn't true or helpful from your own voice. Then, circle or highlight all that God is saying to you!

Give the students some time to do this activity. It might be nice to play some quiet worship music while they write. Be prepared to pray or follow up with kids who may have some hurtful things come up as they write.

Closing: [15 minutes]

As we finish up today, I want to ask you a question:

Why should you want to hear from God? Why does it matter? *Allow response if time.*

Hearing from God reminds us of how real He is. His words are also so life-giving and wonderful, it makes sense that we would want to soak them up. Hearing from God also reminds us that God values us enough to talk to us. It's crazy, but the Creator of the world wants to have a conversation with US! He wants to speak to you even more than you want to hear from Him. Keep listening, and you'll be amazed at how much He has to say.

Lesson 9

In *John 15:15* Jesus said, "Now you are my friends, since I have told you everything the Father told me." Bottom line is: Jesus called you his friend and He's ready and waiting to tell you everything.

Let's pray!

Close in prayer.

We Believe For Kids!

Teacher's Guide

Lesson 10
Worldview

Lesson 10

Doctrinal Statement:

We believe the Bible is God's Word; it is truth. It serves as a trustworthy guide to our everyday lives.

Big Question:

Isn't all truth equal? Who are you to say that your "truth" is right?

Lesson Aim:

To help students examine their worldview, why they believe what they believe, and why it is important to base our worldview on the Word of God rather than society's changing values.

Key Verse:

"And you will know the truth, and the truth will set you free" (John 8:32).

Materials:

Bibles for each student
Student's journals

Worldview

Setup:

Be sure to spend time in prayer this week for your class, asking God to open their eyes to truth. Become familiar with the different worldviews found in the chart. Also be prepared to answer some tough questions, and as often as possible to throw the question back to the student, asking him or her to answer their question in light of what they have learned in the Bible.

Lesson 10

Warming Up: [10 minutes]

Pray together as you begin class. Ask that God would lead your discussion times and open your students' eyes to see truth.

The term "doctrine" simply means a set of beliefs held and taught by a church, political party, or other group.

Why do you think it is so important to take this class, to study "doctrine?" **Allow students to answer.**

Have any of you heard of the term, "worldview?" If so, tell me what you think it is. **Allow students to answer.**

A worldview is how we think about the world. It's a collection of attitudes, values, and expectations about the world around us. Your worldview influences your every thought and action. It affects your choices, how you act in certain situations. It determines how you spend your time and your money. It even helps determine what you decide to do with your life.

For instance, if you believe there is a God who is always watching you, you will most likely make choices you feel would please Him even if that choice means not doing something you really want to do. And if you believe there is a God, a God who knows and loves you, you will be able to be calmer when you encounter difficult challenges.

If you do not believe in any god, you will most likely make choices that work out best for you even if those choices may hurt someone else. And if you do not believe in a god, you may be worried about controlling your future because you may feel as if everything is "up to you" alone.

Going Deeper: [20 minutes]

Look at the worldview featured in your journal.

Divide the class into partners or small groups. Assign each group one worldview to read and summarize in their own words. Then ask each of the groups to share their summary with the class.

Lesson 10

Five Worldviews:

Naturalism—
Atheism; Agnosticism; Existentialism

Reality - The material universe (what we can see, hear, taste, smell, or touch) is all that exists. There are no such things as souls or spirits. Everything is explained by natural law.

Man - Humans are simply a product of evolution. When we die, we cease to exist. All humankind will one day cease to exist.

Truth - Truth is that which can be explained through science. It is what we can explain through our five senses.

Values - No objective values or morals exist. Morals are individual preferences or socially useful behaviors, subject to change.

Important fact:
Our spirit is the nonphysical part of our being.
It's the part of us that holds our emotions and character.
It's the part that will remain alive after our body dies,
the part that connects to God.

Worldview

Pantheism–
Hinduism; Taoism; Buddhism; New Age

Reality - Only the spiritual dimensions exists. Everything we can see, hear, taste, smell, or touch is just an illusion. Spiritual reality is eternal, impersonal, and unknowable. Everything is a part of "God," or "God" is in everything and everyone.

Man - Humans are one with ultimate reality (God). Therefore we are spiritual, eternal, and impersonal. Our belief that we are individuals is just an illusion.

Truth - Truth is an experience of unity with the "oneness" of the universe. Truth is beyond all rational description. Rational thought as we understand it cannot show us reality.

Values - Many pantheistic thinkers believe there is no real distiniction between good and evil. Instead, "unenlightened" behavior is that which fails to understand the unity between us, others, and God.

Lesson 10

Theism –
Christianity; Islam; Judaisim

Reality - An infinite, personal God exists. He created a finite, material world. Reality is both material (what you can see, hear, taste, smell, or touch) and spiritual. The universe as we know it had a beginning and will have an end, but there is an afterlife (life after the life we experience on this earth).

Man - Humans are the unique creation of God. People were created "in the image of God," which means that we are personal, eternal, spiritual, and physical.

Truth - God reveals the truth about Himself (revelation). Truth about the material world is gained by revelation and the five senses in conjuntion with rational thought.

Values - Our moral values are the expression of an absolute moral being.

Worldview

Reality - The world is filled with spirit beings who govern what goes on. Gods and demons are the real reason behind "natural" events. Material things are real, but they have spirits associated with them, and therefore, can be interpreted spiritually.

Man - Humans, like the rest of the creatures on earth, are created by the gods. Often, tribes or races have a special relationship with some gods whom they feel protect them and can punish them.

Truth - Truth about the natural world is discovered through a "shaman," or special, spiritual figure. These figures experience visions telling them what the gods and demons are doing and how they feel.

Values - Moral values take the form of taboos, which are things that irritate or anger various spirits. The "taboos" are different from the idea of "good and evil" because they feel it is just as important to avoid irritating evil spirits as it is good ones.

Lesson 10

Postmodernism

Reality – Reality must be interpreted through our language and cultural "paradigm," or our own framework of experiences.

Man – Humans are a product of their cultural reality or social setting. The idea that people are autonomous (free to govern themselves, able to control their own behavior) is a myth.

Truth – We are free to decide our own truths. Our truth may not apply to other cultural settings. Truth is realative to one's culture. There is no such thing as "absolute truth."

Values – Values are also part of our social and cultural "paradigms," or settings. Tolerance, freedom of expression, inclusion, and refusal to claim to have the truth are the only universal values.

Going Deeper: [continued]

Ask Is there one of these worldviews that you agree with more than others? How would you describe your worldview in your own words? *Have students write their worldview in their journal. Emphasize their worldview does not have to be identical to any on the chart.*

Some people will try to tell you that it does not matter what your worldview is, that all worldviews are equal. They will try to tell you that you cannot know truth. Which worldview would that be? *Allow students to answer.*

Answer = postmodernism

Do you agree with the statement that all truths are equal, or that truth is subjective (whatever we want it to be)? Do you believe it's fine to believe whatever you want to believe? Why or why not?

Allow students to answer without judgment. Keep the tone in your voice non-challenging so that students will feel comfortable answering honestly.

Then say, Let's explore what that concept looks like.

Lesson 10

Let's say I have diabetes. The doctor would normally tell me I need to monitor my blood sugar by balancing my diet and exercise, and often by taking insulin. What would happen if I didn't agree with the doctor's diagnosis and refused to follow his or her advice? *Allow students to answer. Answer = possible death*

If truth is subjective, you should be able to believe whatever you want, right? Then why couldn't I believe I did not have diabetes and thus eat and act accordingly? *Let students articulate: You would die.*

What if I want to believe that I'm a good swimmer even though I've never been in the water? Does my belief that I'm a good swimmer make it true? Of course not!

How many people have driven under the influence of alcohol or other drugs believing they were not impaired and then hurt themselves or others in an accident? It's important that we know the truth regarding our physical bodies, isn't it?

It's even more important to know spiritual truth. Just as a diabetic needs to follow his or her doctor's advice to be healthy, we need to follow spiritual truth so that we can be healthy spiritually. And, as Christians we believe that even though our physical bodies will die someday, our spiritual bodies, our souls, will live forever. We want that to be in the right place!

Worldview

But you might say, "I don't need the Bible or God to tell me what's right and wrong. I'm smart enough to figure that out on my own!"

If that is true, then why do we have so many different viewpoints about so many subjects? People you know have different views about abortion, civil rights, gender identity, sexual matters, marriage, and so many things, and they live their lives according to those beliefs. In fact, you may have already changed your own opinion about some things you believe in.

If time allows, let your students add other issues about which they've heard conflicting views.

This is why it is so important to study doctrine, to know what you believe and why you believe it! What we believe affects the choices we make. And just as an impaired driver's choice to drive not only affects themselves, but others as well, it's the same way with our worldview. What we believe affects ourselves and others because our choices affect ourselves and others.

We have seen that it is important to know the truth. How do we know what the truth is? Let's look back to our doctrinal statement:

"We believe the Bible is God's Word; it is truth. It serves as a trustworthy guide to our everyday lives."

A follower of Christ's worldview relies on the fact that God's Word is truth, just as we learned in lessons 1 through 3. The Bible is the Word of God; it is truth. The fact that the Word of God is truth was Jesus' worldview, and He acted on that belief.

Ask a volunteer to read Philippians 2:7-8

Philippians 2:7-8:
You must have the same attitude that Christ Jesus had. Though he was God he did not think of equality with God as something to cling to. Instead, he gave up his divine privileges; he took the humble position of a slave and was born as a human being. When he appeared in human form, he humbled himself in obedience to God and died a criminal's death on a cross.

How did Jesus' worldview affect others?

Answer = provided us salvation

How could your worldview affect others?
Allow students to answer.

Worldview

Ask another volunteer to read Philippians 2:9-11.

Philippians 2:9-11:
Therefore, God elevated him to the place of highest honor and gave him the name above all other names, that at the name of Jesus every knee should bow, in heaven and on earth and under the earth, and every tongue declare that Jesus Christ is Lord, to the glory of God the Father.

How did Jesus' worldview affect Himself?
God took Him to heaven and elevated him to the place of highest honor.

Activation: [15 minutes]

Jesus' disciples hung out with Him for three years. They ate together, traveled together, prayed together, and ministered together. They did everything together. They knew Jesus well, and they believed in Him, so much so that all but one of them were killed because they refused to renounce Him.

They viewed the world through the lens of Jesus. That worldview affected their choices, and all of them spent their lives serving others and sharing the gospel them.

Lesson 10

Divide into groups of approximately three to four students. Give each group one of the following scenarios (or one of your own) and ask them to decide how a person from some of the other worldviews might respond to that situation. Remind them that even though someone has a different worldview, that doesn't mean they always make bad choices.

First scenario:

A new student walks into the lunchroom. It is obvious from the student's clothing and their accent that they have recently arrived from a different country. Several students are making fun of him/her.

Second scenario:

The person's friend tries to get them to engage in inappropriate behavior, assuring him/her that no one will find out.
Depending on your classroom situation, you could more clearly define the inappropriate behavior, such as cheating, bullying someone, sexual behavior, or stealing.

Third scenario:

A schoolteacher tells the class that the values their parents or churches taught them are old-fashioned, that the student should be able to do whatever they want with their own bodies, even if it means going against things their parents have taught them (such as a boy dressing like a girl or vice versa).

Closing: [15 minutes]

Ask Have you ever thought about your own worldview? Has it changed since the beginning of class? If so, how?

Encourage two or three students to answer. Ask them all to review their own worldview that they wrote in their journals and consider if they want to change anything.

Sometimes we may say we adhere to a Christian worldview, believing that the Bible is truth, but our choices do not reflect that belief. Sometimes we say we believe in God, but we act like we don't. We may be more afraid of what our friends think about us than what God thinks about us. Even now, in this room, some of us are thinking more about what other students are thinking about us than what God thinks. Yikes!

Ask God to show you times that you have not acted like you believe what you say you believe. Let Him know you are sorry for those actions and ask Him to forgive you. Ask the Holy Spirit to give you the courage to live out your beliefs.

Pray for students before dismissing.

Lesson 10

We Believe For Kids!

Teacher's Guide

Lesson 11
Book
Review

Lesson 11

Doctrinal Statement:

Review all doctrinal statements that have been covered in this book.

Review Big Questions:

Review all Big Questions that have been asked in this book.

Lesson Aim:

Review all lessons that have been covered in this book.

Materials:

A physical Bible for each student
Student's journals
Whiteboard or butcher paper with markers

Review Lesson 1 - 3: The Bible

Doctrinal Statement:

We believe the Bible is God's Word; it is truth. It serves as a trustworthy guide to our everyday lives.

Key Verses:

2 Timothy 3:16:
All Scripture is inspired by God and is useful to teach us what is true and to make us realize what is wrong in our lives. It corrects us when we are wrong and teaches us to do what is right.

Hebrews 4:12:
For the word of God is alive and powerful. It is sharper than the sharpest two-edged sword, cutting between soul and spirit, between joint and marrow. It exposes our innermost thoughts and desires.

Psalm 119:105:
Your word is a lamp to guide my feet and a light for my path.

Main Points:

- The Bible is ***100 percent the creation of human authors but also 100 percent inspired by God***. God himself breathed this Truth into existence. He planted the words in the minds of many writers, helping them

Lesson 11

create this book that is capable of guiding us when we are lost, revealing God's love for us and transforming our lives.

- There are **two main sections: the Old Testament and the New Testament.** The Old Testament is the larger of the two testaments and includes everything from the creation of the world until just a few hundred years before Jesus. The first four books of the New Testament are called the gospels. They are firsthand accounts of the life of Jesus. The rest of the New Testament recounts how the early followers of Jesus were instructed to live and follow Jesus' teachings.

- The Bible was **written over a time span of 1,600 years by at least 40 authors**, which included kings, scholars, tax collectors, philosophers, fishermen, statesmen, poets, historians, teachers, prophets, and doctors.

- The Bible **contains different types of literature: history, poetry, prophecy, and even letters**. More than 300 prophetic details (details mentioned before they actually happened) about Jesus' life found in the Old Testament came true, such as the fact that He would be born of a virgin, His birthplace would be Bethlehem, and that He would be crucified between two thieves.

- **The Bible is powerful**. God's Word is our main weapon for battle. It's part of the armor of God (*Ephesians 6:17*).

- **"Scripture"** is another word for **"Bible"**. Scripture is inspired or "God-breathed." When God sent Jesus to us, it was another way for Him to send His very words to us. When Jesus spoke, He spoke God's words. When we read the Bible, we read God's words.

Book Review

- *The Bible is personal.* If you want to know who God made you to be or what He thinks of you, this is the only book you need.

- The Bible *isn't something our brain can understand all by itself.* It was written not just for our brains, but also for our spirit. The most powerful thing you can do to help yourself understand God's Word is to invite the Holy Spirit to read it with you.

- Our spirit is the *nonphysical part of our being*. It's the part of us that holds our emotions and character. It's the part that will remain alive after our body dies, the part that connects to God.

- There are so many great ways to read the Bible. This lesson gave you three ideas: reading plans or *devotionals*, reading *one book of the Bible at a time*, or *asking the Holy Spirit to guide you to a passage*.

- Regardless of what method you choose, there is one thing that is so important: *Journal what you read and what God speaks* to you through your reading. One popular way to journal is the *SOAP* method: Scripture - Write down the Scripture passage you read. Observation - What do you notice about the verse? Do you have questions? Application - How might this verse or story apply to your life or what you're going through today? Pray - Ask God if there's anything else He wants you to know and write down anything you hear Him saying. Thank Him for what He has spoken to you.

Lesson 11

Review Lesson 5-7:
God the Father; God the Son; God the Holy Spirit

Doctrinal Statement:

We believe God is the eternal, all-powerful, all-knowing, everywhere-present, and unchangeable Creator of all, who is also the God of love, mercy, and compassion.

We believe Jesus is co-Creator with the Father. Conceived miraculously, He is all human and all God. He died and rose again to make possible our relationship with God. Now He is in heaven with the Father praying for us.

We believe in God the Holy Spirit, co-Creator with the Father and the Son. He helps us know when we've done wrong, make good decisions, and learn what is true. He gives us power and the tools to be like Jesus.

Key Verses:

1 John 3:1: See how very much our Father loves us, for he calls us his children, and that is what we are! But the people who belong to this world don't recognize that we are God's children because they don't know him.

Romans 5:8: But God showed his great love for us by sending Christ to die for us while we were still sinners.

John 14:16: And I will ask the Father, and he will give you another Advocate, who will never leave you.

Book Review

Main Points:

- There is only one God, but He shows himself to us as three persons united in one Godhead *(Matthew 28:19)*. **God the Father, God the Son, and God the Holy Spirit**.

- **We are God's children** *(Romans 8:16)*. **We are God's creation**, created for his purpose. God made us for a reason; we were not created by chance *(Isaiah 64:8)*. We are special.

- **We are made in God's image**, so we share some of His attributes or qualities. Examples: goodness, mercy, and love.

- There are some qualities that are unique to God alone. **God is a spirit**. **God is omnipotent** *(Isaiah 40:28-31)*. **God is omniscient** *(Psalms 139:1-6)*. **God is omnipresent** *(Psalms 139:7-12)*. God is holy *(1 Peter 1:16)*.

- **Jesus was born to an earthly mother, which makes Him fully human and He was born to a Heavenly Father, which makes Him fully God.** Jesus told us in Scripture that He and the Father are the same. They are the same person fulfilling different roles *(John 14:9-10)*.

- **God and his word cannot be separated; they are one and the same.** So, to say the word became flesh and made his home among us is to say God himself came in human form to live with us *(John 1:1; 1:14)*.

- **Jesus becoming human enabled us to see what God is like**; it helped us to relate to Him.

Lesson 11

- *A sin nature, our natural desire to do what is wrong, was passed down from Adam and Eve into all humans born thereafter* (Romans 3:23). This was not what God intended. God's original plan was to have a close relationship with us. He made us in his image and gave us power over all things, but Adam and Eve's sin separated us from God.

- *God wanted to bring us back to Him, but there was a price that had to be paid.* The Bible states that the wages for sin is death (Romans 6:23).

- God looked everywhere but *there was no one who was sinless – not one person (Psalm 53:2-3; Romans 3:10-12).*

- *Jesus Christ, God's Son, was crucified on the cross for our sins.* Christ later rose from the dead and ascended to heaven. He defeated sin and death, and removed the distance between people and God. Now we can have a relationship with God our Father through his Son, Jesus Christ.

- *Everyone who believes in Jesus Christ, who died on the cross for our sins and rose from the dead, shall be saved.* But first we need to ask God to forgive us for all the wrong things we have done and turn away from doing wrong.

- *Now, when God, our Heavenly Father, sees us He sees the righteousness of his Son, Jesus Christ.* This means that we are now in right standing with God but only through Jesus Christ.

Book Review

- *When we accept Jesus Christ as our Savior, his Spirit comes and lives inside our hearts.* His Spirit is our Helper.

- *The Holy Spirit was sent by God to carry out His will in and through us.* He is at work in our hearts to make us better children of God. He tries to prevent us from doing what is wrong. He prays for us and helps us with our weaknessess *(Romans 8:26).* The Holy Spirit helps us to love others *(Colossians 1:8)* and to understand God better *(Ephesians 1:17).*

- *We can relate to the Holy Spirit as a person,* not a thing, because the Holy Spirit can teach, pray, love, and feel sadness just like we do *(Isaiah 63:10).*

- The Bible states that the Holy Spirit produces good qualities, or "fruit," in our lives: *love, joy, peace, patience, kindness, goodness, faithfulness, gentleness, and self-control (Galatians 5:22-23).*

Lesson 11

Review Lesson 9-10:
God Speaks; Worldview

Doctrinal Statement:

We believe that even though God is the eternal, all-powerful, all-knowing, everywhere-present, and unchangeable Creator of all, He wants a relationship with each one of us.

We believe the Bible is God's Word; it is truth. It serves as a trustworthy guide to our everyday lives.

Key Verses:

John 10:27:
My sheep listen to my voice; I know them, and they follow me.

John 8:32:
And you will know the truth, and the truth will set you free.

Main Points:

- **God doesn't just speak to adults; He also speaks to kids.** Jesus told his disciples that his entire kingdom belongs to kids *(Luke 18:16)*, so there's nothing in his kingdom that doesn't include you. His gifts, his voice, his Word, his Holy Spirit — God wants you to experience all of it!

154

Book Review

- Examples of people in the Bible hearing from God: Samuel *(1 Samuel 3:1-10)*; David *(Psalm 40:3)*; Josheph *(Genesis 37:5-11)*; Daniel *(Daniel 7:1)*; Mary *(Luke 1: 26, 46-55)*. God spoke not only to adults but to kids, and He not only spoke to people in the Bible, He speaks to us today! *(John 8:47; John 10:27; Jeremiah 33:3; Deuteronomy 30:14)*.

- *God's words are living and active.* They are powerful, transformative, sweet, perfect, true, enlightening, helpful, kind, and lovely.

- *If we don't feel better or cleaner or more free after hearing something, it's not God.* Even his corrections are sweet and lead us toward freedom and joy. He will never lie to you, or be cruel to you, or hurt you in any way.

- It is challenging to learn how to tell the difference between God's voice and other voices that influence our lives. *The three most common voices we hear are: God's voice, Satan's voice, and our own voice.*

- *Satan is our enemy.* Scripture says he's a deceiver and an accuser, so when he speaks he will try to lie, trick, confuse, anger, blame, or scare you. If you're hearing something that makes you feel those emotions, it's often Satan who is behind it.

- *Our voice speaks to us about our own wants and desires.* It's interested in our comfort and is pretty self-serving. If our thoughts are consumed with what's best for us and what we want or wish, odds are it's our own voice speaking to us.

Lesson 11

- The term "**doctrine**" simply means a set of beliefs held and taught by a church, political party, or other group.

- **Worldview is how we think about the world**. It's a collection of attitudes, values, and expectations about the world around us. Your worldview influences your every thought and action. It affects your choices, how you act in certain situations. It determines how you spend your time and your money. It even helps determine what you decide to do with your life.

- **Five Worldviews: *Naturalism*** (Atheism; Agnosticism; Existentialism); ***Pantheism*** (Hinduism; Taoism; Buddhism; New Age); ***Theism*** (Christianity; Islam; Judaisim); ***Spiritism & Polytheism***; ***Postmodernism***.

- **Naturalism** (Atheism; Agnosticism; Existentialism) - The material universe (what we can see, hear, taste, smell, or touch) is all that exists. There are no such things as souls or spirits. Everything is explained by natural law. Humans are simply a product of evolution. When we die, we cease to exist. All humankind will one day cease to exist. Truth is that which can be explained through science. It is what we can explain through our five senses. No objective values or morals exist. Morals are individual preferences or socially useful behaviors, subject to change.

- **Pantheism** (Hinduism; Taoism; Buddhism; New Age) - Only the spiritual dimensions exists. Everything we can see, hear, taste, smell, or touch is just an illusion. Spiritual reality is eternal, impersonal, and unknowable. Everything is a part of "God," or "God" is in everything and everyone. Humans are one with ultimate reality (God). Therefore we are spiritual, eternal, and impersonal. Our belief that we are individuals is just an illusion. Truth is an experience of unity with the "oneness" of the universe. Truth is beyond all rational description. Rational thought as we understand it cannot show us reality. Many pantheistic thinkers believe there is no real distiniction between good and evil. Instead, "unenlightened" behavior is that which fails to understand the unity between us, others, and God.

- **Theism** (Christianity; Islam; Judaisim) - An infinite, personal God exists. He created a finite, material world. Reality is both material (what you can see, hear, taste, smell, or touch) and spiritual. The universe as we know it had a beginning and will have an end, but there is an afterlife (life after the life we experience on this earth). Humans are the unique creation of God. People were created "in the image of God," which means that we are personal, eternal, spiritual, and physical. God reveals the truth about Himself (revelation). Truth about the material world is gained by revelation and the five senses in conjunction with rational thought. Our moral values are the expression of an absolute moral being.

- **Spiritism & Polytheism** - The world is filled with spirit beings who govern what goes on. Gods and demons are the real reason behind "natural" events. Material things are real, but they have spirits associated with them, and therefore, can be interpreted spiritually. Humans, like the rest of the creatures on earth, are created by the gods. Often, tribes or races have a special relationship with some gods whom they feel protect them and can punish them. Truth about the natural world is discovered through a "shaman," or special, spiritual figure. These figures experience visions telling them what the gods and demons are doing and how they feel. Moral values take the form of taboos, which are things that irritate or anger various spirits. The "taboos" are different from the idea of "good and evil" because they feel it is just as important to avoid irritating evil spirits as it is good ones.

- **Postmodernism** - Reality must be interpreted through our language and cultural "paradigm," or our own framework of experiences. Humans are a product of their cultural reality or social setting. The idea that people are autonomous (free to govern themselves, able to control their own behavior) is a myth. We are free to decide our own truths. Our truth may not apply to other cultural settings. Truth is relative to one's culture. There is no such thing as "absolute truth." Values are also part of our social and cultural "paradigms," or settings. Tolerance, freedom of expression, inclusion, and refusal to claim to have the truth are the only universal values.

- If truth is subjective, you should be able to believe whatever you want, but what about things like believing your doctor's diagnosis and treatment options? Or people that drive under the influence of drugs or alcohol because they "believe" they are fine?

Book Review

- It's even more important to know spiritual truth.

- A follower of Christ's worldview relies on the fact that **God's Word is truth,** just as we learned in Lessons 1 through 3. The Bible is the Word of God; it is truth. The fact that the Word of God is truth was Jesus' worldview, and He acted on that belief.

- Jesus's worldview affected us becaue it provides us with salvation when we accept Him as our Savior. Our worldview can affect others because *we can either point people to Jesus or away from him.*

Lesson 11

Book Review Jepordy:

Use this game to test your student's knowledge of the materials.

Instructions for Playing Jeopardy:

- Play individually or in groups

- On a whiteboard or butcher paper, write the following categories across the top along with the point values going down.

The Bible	God the Father	God the Son	God the HS	God Speaks	Worldview	Did you Know
100	100	100	100	100	100	100
200	200	200	200	200	200	200
300	300	300	300	300	300	300
400	400	400	400	400	400	400
500	500	500	500	500	500	500

- Have a student/team pick a category and point value.

- Read the corresponding question out loud and allow the student to answer (answer in the form of a question, "What is...").

- If they get the answer correct they/their team gets the points. If they get it incorrect, the opposing team gets a chance to answer for the points.

- Cross off the answered category/point value on the

board and allow the next student to choose the next category/ point.

- The team with the most points after all the questions have been answered wins.

Notes and Suggestions for Playing:

- Establish a time limit for each question to be answered.

- You could allow the team to discuss each answer before declaring their offical answer or make student answer on their own.

- Teams should answer the questions in order (100, 200, 300, etc) before going to the next one in that category. They can switch between categories but not skip point values.

- Instead of allowing only one team to answer at a time, you could have one team pick the category but then allow each team to "race" to answer. Teams can use noise makers, buzzers, or literally run to the front of the room to signal they want to answer. Whoever is heard first or gets to the front of the room first gets to answer.

- Award a prize to the winning team, or get something for everyone!

- Make this a fun class. Bring treats or come up with other games to do to review.

Lesson 11

Jepordy Questions:

Here are the category questions and their answers for the game.

The Bible:

100 - Fill in the blank: The Bible is 100 percent the creation of human authors but also 100 percent _____ by God.
[answer: What is "inspired?"]

200 - Name the two main sections of the Bible.
[answer: What is the "Old Testament and New Testament?"]

300 - The first four books of the New Testament are called the _____.
[answer: What are "the gospels?"]

400 - We talked about how the word of God can be a weapon against our enemies and it can tell you about who God made you to be. What were the two words that we used to describe the word of God?
[answer: What are "powerful and personal?"]

500 - We discussed an important journaling method. What is it called and what does it stand for?
[answer: What is "SOAP - Scripture, Observation, Application, Prayer?"]

Book Review

God the Father:

100 - Fill in the blank: We are made in God's image, so we share some of his _____.
[answer: What are "attributes or qualities?"]

200 - This term means that God cannot tolerate sin.
[answer: What is "holy?"]

300 - This term means that God knows everything.
[answer: What is "omniscient?"]

400 - This term means that God is all powerful.
[answer: What is "omnipotent?"]

500 - This term means that God is everywhere.
[answer: What is "omnipresent?"]

Lesson 11

God the Son:

100 - Fill in the blanks: Jesus was born of an earthly mother and a Heavenly Father. This makes Jesus fully _____ and fully _____. *[answer: What is "human and God?"]*

200 - This natural desire to do what is wrong separates us from God. *[answer: What is "sin nature?"]*

300 - Fill in the blanks: The Bible states that the wages of sin is _____. *[answer: What is "death?"]*

400 - Everyone who asks God to forgive their sins and believes that Jesus did these two things, shall be saved. *[answers: What is "died on the cross and rose from the dead?"]*

500 - God sent Jesus to die for our sins for what purpose? *[answer: What is "restore our relationship with Him?"]*

Book Review

God the Holy Spirit:

100 - Another name for the Holy Spirit is what?
[answer: What is "helper?"]

200 - What are two things the Holy Spirit was sent by God to carry out in and through us? *[possible answers: What is "make us better children of God," "prevent us from doing what is wrong," "pray for us," "help us to love overs," "help us to understand God better?"]*

300 - Fill in the blank: Since the Holy Spirit can teach, pray, love, and feel sadness just like we do, we can relate to Him as a _____, not a thing. *[answer: What is "person?"]*

400 - When does the Holy Spirit come and live inside our hearts?
[asnwer: What is "when we accept Jesus Christ as our Savior?"]

500 - Name the nine fruits of the Spirit according to Galatians 5:22-23. *[answer: What is "love, joy, peace, patience, kindness, goodness, faithfulness, gentleness, and self-control?"]*

Lesson 11

God Speaks:

100 - Fill in the blank: God doesn't just speak to adults; He also speaks to _____. *[answer: What are "kids?"]*

200 - Give three examples from our lessons of young people who heard from God. *[possible answers: Who is "Samuel, David, Joseph, Daniel, Mary?"]*

300 - There are two other voices that may influence our lives. What are they? *[answer: What are "Satan's voice and my voice"?]*

400 - What are at least 2 characteristics of God's word? *[possible answers: What are "living," "active," "powerful," "transformative," "sweet," "perfect," "true," "enlightening," "helpful," "kind," "lovely?"]*

500 - What are some ways we know that it is God's voice speaking to us? *[possible answers: What is "we will feel better, cleaner, more free," "we will have more freedom and joy?"]*

Book Review

Worldview:

100 - This term means a set of beliefs held and taught by a church, political party, or other group. *[answer: What is "doctrine?"]*

200 - This term is a collection of attitudes, values, and expectations about the world around you. It is how we think about the world. *[answer: What is "worldview?"]*

300 - This worldview says that the material world (what we can see, hear, taste, smell, or touch) is all that exists. There is no such thing as spirits or souls. Everything is explained by natural law. When we die, we cease to exist. It includes religions like Atheism, Agnosticism, and Existentialism. *[answer: What is "Naturalism?"]*

400 - This worldview says that everything we can see, hear, taste, smell, or touch is just an illusion. Only the spiritual dimension exists. Everything is part of "God" or "God" is in everything and everyone. It includes religions like, Hinduism, Taoism, Buddhism, and New Age. *[answer: What is "Pantheism?"]*

500 - This worldview says that an infinite, personal God exists. He created a finite, material world and both material and spiritual realities exist. The universe as we know it had a beginning and will end, but there is an afterlife. It includes religions like, Chrisianity, Islam, and Judaisim. *[answer: What is "Theism?"]*

Lesson 11

Did you Know:

100 - Which book is the best-selling book of the year every year?

[answer: What is "the Bible?"]

200 - There are how many individual books that make up the whole Bible (both Old and New Testament)?

[answer: What is "66 books?"]

300 - This term refers to the nonphysical part of our being. It is the part that holds our emotions and character. It will remain alive after our body dies, the part that connects to God.

[answer: What is "our spirit?"]

400 - This animal can hear at frequencies 20 times lower than humans. It isn't just their ears that perceive sound...

[possibe answer: What is "elephant?"]

500 - What is one thing that you learned during this class that you didn't know before you started?

[answers will vary based on the student. Award points if they answer thoughtfully.]

Appendix

Skit-Lesson 1

Two characters: **Ralph and Abby**

[Abby finds Ralph typing on his cell phone. Abby is wise, knowledgeable, and compassionate. Ralph finishes sending a post of some kind, then starts a conversation about getting some likes already.]

Ralph: Hey Abby, are you going to like my post? I mean, how many dogs can skateboard like that?

Abby: That is pretty cool. You'll get TONS of likes! [Abby pulls out her phone and likes his post.]

[Transition] **Abby:** Another thing that must get a lot of likes is a book I've been waiting for at the library. It has a really long waiting list.

Ralph: I usually wait for the movie, unless the book is a comic book!

Abby: That's funny. Do you know the *Diary of a Wimpy Kid* series? Guess how many copies of those books have been sold?

Ralph: I don't know… one hundred thousand?

Abby: No higher!

Ralph: Five hundred thousand!

Abby: Higher!

Ralph: [impressed] One million.

Abby: Two HUNDRED million!! Guess how many copies of *Narnia* have been sold?

Ralph: I don't know…

Abby: 100 million! *Lord of the Rings* – 150 million! *The Harry Potter series* – 500 million. And guess what else! Over five BILLION copies of the

Bible have been sold! Every year 100 million copies of the Bible are sold or given away. In fact, it's been translated into more languages than any other book in history! Did you know the *YouVersion Bible App* has been downloaded more than 250 million times, in 1,000 languages?! The Bible is the best-selling book of the year every year!!!

Ralph: Wow!! I bet no one knows that! I'm going to have to make a new post... [He types while talking out loud]. Hey everyone, I bet you didn't know that the Bible is the best-selling book? More than five BILLION copies... [His voice fades.]

END

Appendix

Skit-Lesson 5

Two characters: **Joseph and Juan**

Joseph: Juan, my dad is so annoying!

Juan: Why? What did he do?

Joseph: He expects me to be perfect all the time. When I mess up, he gets upset. I'm not Superman!

Juan: You mean Super Kid!

Joseph: Come on Juan, I'm being serious.

Juan: Okay, sorry. My dad is like that too. He says he pushes me to do well because he loves me. It's a parent thing.

Joseph: I guess (sigh). My dad always complains that I watch TV too much or play video games. He says [say in a mockingly stern way], "Learn something, Joseph. You were born for a reason, you know! You were not born to sit around all day doing nothing." I was born for a reason?! Nobody told me about the reason.

Juan: I guess dads can be a bit annoying, or downright scary at times, but sometimes dads can be cool.

Joseph: Ugh!

Juan: But still, I know my dad loves me because he is the first person to run to my rescue if I am hurt. If I have a problem, I can talk to him about it. Sometimes he tells me that I need to make better choices. I swear he has eyes in the back of his head. He seems to know every time I mess up!

Joseph: But why do dads have to care about everything we do? Why can't they just leave us alone sometimes?

Juan: I know, right? It's annoying, but at least your dad cares. Angela's dad took off months ago and she hasn't heard from him since. He doesn't have any idea what she is doing. She wishes he cared enough to at least check in once in a while.

Joseph: Yeah (sigh), I guess you're right. [Joseph gets up to leave.] Later, Juan. I am off to have a man-to-man talk with my dad.

Juan: You mean man to boy!

Joseph: Ugh! [waves goodbye]

END

Certificate

For an 8.5"X11", downloadable copy of this certificate, go to:

openbible.org/WB4K

OPEN BIBLE.
CHURCHES

Certificate of Completion

Awarded to

_____

We Believe For Kids

Book One - Who Is God?

Teacher/Pastor: _____   Date: _____

OPEN BIBLE.
CHURCHES

Made in the USA
Columbia, SC
04 October 2021

46392228R00102